MASTER THE™ DSST®

Fundamentals
of
Counseling
Exam

About Peterson's

Peterson's has been your trusted educational publisher for more than 50 years. It's a milestone we're quite proud of, as we continue to offer the most accurate, dependable, high-quality educational content in the field, providing you with everything you need to succeed. No matter where you are on your academic or professional path, you can rely on Peterson's for its books, online information, expert test-prep tools, the most up-to-date education exploration data, and the highest quality career success resources—everything you need to achieve your education goals. For our complete line of products, visit **www.petersons.com**.

For more information, contact Peterson's, 4380 S. Syracuse St., Suite 200, Denver, CO 80237; 800-338-3282 Ext. 54229; or visit us online at **www.petersons.com**.

ISBN-13: 978-0-7689-4450-1

Printed in the United States of America

10 9 8 7 6 5 4 3 2 1   23 22 21

Contents

Before You Begin

HOW THIS BOOK IS ORGANIZED

Peterson's *Master the*™ *DSST® Fundamentals of Counseling Exam*
provides a diagnostic test, subject-matter review, and a post-test.

- **Diagnostic Test**—Twenty multiple-choice questions, followed by an answer key with detailed answer explanations
- **Assessment Grid**—A chart designed to help you identify areas that you need to focus on based on your test results
- **Subject-Matter Review**—General overview of the exam subject, followed by a review of the relevant topics and terminology covered on the exam
- **Post-test**—Sixty multiple-choice questions, followed by an answer key and detailed answer explanations

The purpose of the diagnostic test is to help you figure out what you know—or don't know. The 20 multiple-choice questions are similar to the ones found on the DSST exam, and they should provide you with a good idea of what to expect. Once you take the diagnostic test, check your answers to see how you did. Included with each correct answer is a brief explanation regarding why a specific answer is correct, and in many cases, why other options are incorrect. Use the assessment grid to identify the questions you miss so that you can spend more time reviewing that information later. As with any exam, knowing your weak spots greatly improves your chances of success.

Following the diagnostic test is a subject-matter review. The review summarizes the various topics covered on the DSST exam. Key terms are defined; important concepts are explained; and when appropriate, examples are provided. As you read the review, some of the information may seem familiar while other information may seem foreign. Again, take note of the unfamiliar because that will most likely cause you problems on the actual exam.

After studying the subject-matter review, you should be ready for the post-test. The post-test contains sixty multiple-choice items, and it will serve as a dry run for the real DSST exam. There are complete answer explanations at the end of the test.

OTHER DSST® PRODUCTS BY PETERSON'S

Books, flashcards, practice tests, and videos available online at **www.petersons.com/testprep/dsst**

- A History of the Vietnam War
- Art of the Western World
- Astronomy
- Business Mathematics
- Business Ethics and Society
- Civil War and Reconstruction
- Computing and Information Technology
- Criminal Justice
- Environmental Science
- Ethics in America
- Ethics in Technology
- Foundations of Education
- Fundamentals of College Algebra
- Fundamentals of Counseling
- Fundamentals of Cybersecurity
- General Anthropology
- Health and Human Development
- History of the Soviet Union
- Human Resource Management

- Introduction to Business
- Introduction to Geography
- Introduction to Geology
- Introduction to Law Enforcement
- Introduction to World Religions
- Lifespan Developmental Psychology
- Math for Liberal Arts
- Management Information Systems
- Money and Banking
- Organizational Behavior
- Personal Finance
- Principles of Advanced English Composition
- Principles of Finance
- Principles of Public Speaking
- Principles of Statistics
- Principles of Supervision
- Substance Abuse
- Technical Writing

Like what you see? Get unlimited access to Peterson's full catalog of DSST practice tests, instructional videos, flashcards, and more for **75% off the first month!** Go to **www.petersons.com/testprep/dsst** and use coupon code **DSST2020** at checkout. Offer expires July 1, 2021.

Chapter 1

All About the DSST® Exam

WHAT IS DSST®?

Previously known as the DANTES Subject Standardized Tests, the DSST program provides the opportunity for individuals to earn college credit for what they have learned outside of the traditional classroom. Accepted or administered at more than 1,900 colleges and universities nationwide and approved by the American Council on Education (ACE), the DSST program enables individuals to use the knowledge they have acquired outside the classroom to accomplish their educational and professional goals.

WHY TAKE A DSST® EXAM?

DSST exams offer a way for you to save both time and money in your quest for a college education. Why enroll in a college course in a subject you already understand? For more than 30 years, the DSST program has offered the perfect solution for individuals who are knowledgeable in a specific subject and want to save both time and money. A passing score on a DSST exam provides physical evidence to universities of proficiency in a specific subject. More than 1,900 accredited and respected colleges and universities across the nation award undergraduate credit for passing scores on DSST exams. With the DSST program, individuals can shave months off the time it takes to earn a degree.

The DSST program offers numerous advantages for individuals in all stages of their educational development:

- Adult learners
- College students
- Military personnel

Adult learners desiring college degrees face unique circumstances—demanding work schedules, family responsibilities, and tight budgets. Yet adult learners also have years of valuable work experience that can frequently be applied toward a degree through the DSST program. For example, adult learners with on-the-job experience in business and management might be able to skip the Business 101 courses if they earn passing marks on DSST exams such as Introduction to Business and Principles of Supervision.

Adult learners can put their prior learning into action and move forward with more advanced course work. Adults who have never enrolled in a college course may feel a little uncertain about their abilities. If this describes your situation, then sign up for a DSST exam and see how you do. A passing score may be the boost you need to realize your dream of earning a degree. With family and work commitments, adult learners often feel they lack the time to attend college. The DSST program provides adult learners with the unique opportunity to work toward college degrees without the time constraints of semester-long course work. DSST exams take two hours or less to complete. In one weekend, you could earn credit for multiple college courses.

The DSST exams also benefit students who are already enrolled in a college or university. With college tuition costs on the rise, most students face financial challenges. The fee for each DSST exam starts at $100 (plus administration fees charged by some testing facilities)—significantly less than the $750 average cost of a 3-hour college class. Maximize tuition assistance by taking DSST exams for introductory or mandatory course work. Once you earn a passing score on a DSST exam, you are free to move on to higher-level course work in that subject matter, take desired electives, or focus on courses in a chosen major.

Not only do college students and adult learners profit from DSST exams, but military personnel reap the benefits as well. If you are a member of the armed services at home or abroad, you can initiate your post-military career by taking DSST exams in areas with which you have experience. Military personnel can gain credit anywhere in the world, thanks to the fact that almost all of the tests are available through the internet at designated testing locations. DSST testing facilities are located at more than 500 military installations, so service members on active duty can get a jump-start on a post-military career with the DSST program. As an additional incentive, DANTES (Defense Activity for Non-Traditional Education Support) provides funding for DSST test fees for eligible members of the military.

More than 30 subject-matter tests are available in the fields of Business, Humanities, Math, Physical Science, Social Sciences, and Technology.

Available DSST® Exams

Business	Social Sciences
Business Ethics and Society	A History of the Vietnam War
Business Mathematics	Art of the Western World
Computing and Information Technology	Criminal Justice
Human Resource Management	Foundations of Education
Introduction to Business	Fundamentals of Counseling
Management Information Systems	General Anthropology
Money and Banking	History of the Soviet Union
Organizational Behavior	Introduction to Geography
Personal Finance	Introduction to Law Enforcement
Principles of Finance	Lifespan Developmental Psychology
Principles of Supervision	Substance Abuse
	The Civil War and Reconstruction
Humanities	**Physical Sciences**
Ethics in America	Astronomy
Introduction to World Religions	Environmental Science
Principles of Advanced English Composition	Health and Human Development
Principles of Public Speaking	Introduction to Geology
Math	**Technology**
Fundamentals of College Algebra	Ethics in Technology
Math for Liberal Arts	Fundamentals of Cybersecurity
Principles of Statistics	Technical Writing

As you can see from the table, the DSST program covers a wide variety of subjects. However, it is important to ask two questions before registering for a DSST exam.

1. Which universities or colleges award credit for passing DSST exams?
2. Which DSST exams are the most relevant to my desired degree and my experience?

Knowing which universities offer DSST credit is important. In all likelihood, a college in your area awards credit for DSST exams, but find out before taking an exam by contacting the university directly. Then review the list of DSST exams to determine which ones are most relevant to the degree you are seeking and to your base of knowledge. Schedule an appointment with your college adviser to determine which exams best fit your degree program and which college courses the DSST exams can replace. Advisers should also be able to tell you the minimum score required on the DSST exam to receive university credit.

DSST® TEST CENTERS

You can find DSST testing locations in community colleges and universities across the country. Check the DSST website (**www.getcollegecredit. com**) for a location near you or contact your local college or university to find out if the school administers DSST exams. Keep in mind that some universities and colleges administer DSST exams only to enrolled students. DSST testing is available to men and women in the armed services at more than 500 military installations around the world.

HOW TO REGISTER FOR A DSST® EXAM

Once you have located a nearby DSST testing facility, you need to contact the testing center to find out the exam administration schedule. Many centers are set up to administer tests via the internet, while others use printed materials. Almost all DSST exams are available as online tests, but the method used depends on the testing center. The cost for each DSST exam starts at $100, and many testing locations charge a fee to cover their costs for administering the tests. Credit cards are the only accepted payment method for taking online DSST exams. Credit card, certified check, and money order are acceptable payment methods for paper-and-pencil tests.

Test takers are allotted two score reports—one mailed to them and another mailed to a designated college or university, if requested. Online tests generate unofficial scores at the end of the test session, while individuals taking paper tests must wait four to six weeks for score reports.

PREPARING FOR A DSST® EXAM

Even though you are knowledgeable in a certain subject matter, you should still prepare for the test to ensure you achieve the highest score possible. The first step in studying for a DSST exam is to find out what will be on the specific test you have chosen. Information regarding test content is located on the DSST fact sheets, which can be downloaded at no cost from **www.getcollegecredit.com**. Each fact sheet outlines the topics covered on a subject-matter test, as well as the approximate percentage assigned to each topic. For example, questions on the Fundamentals of Counseling exam are distributed in the following way: Historical Development–5%, Counselor Roles and Functions–23%, The Counseling Relationship–12%, Theoretical Approaches–24%, Social and Cultural Foundations–12%, Career Development–6%, Human Growth and Development–8%, and Assessment and Appraisal Techniques 10%.

In addition to the breakdown of topics on a DSST exam, the fact sheet also lists recommended reference materials. If you do not own the recommended books, then check college bookstores. Avoid paying high prices for new textbooks by looking online for used textbooks. Don't panic if you are unable to locate a specific textbook listed on the fact sheet; the textbooks are merely recommendations. Instead, search for comparable books used in university courses on the specific subject. Current editions are ideal, and it is a good idea to use at least two references when studying for a DSST exam. Of course, the subject matter provided in this book will be a sufficient review for most test takers. However, if you need additional information, then it is a good idea to have some of the reference materials at your disposal when preparing for a DSST exam.

Fact sheets include other useful information in addition to a list of reference materials and topics. Each fact sheet includes subject-specific sample questions like those you will encounter on the DSST exam. The sample questions provide an idea of the types of questions you can expect on the exam. Test questions are multiple-choice with one correct answer and three incorrect choices.

The fact sheet also includes information about the number of credit hours ACE has recommended be awarded by colleges for a passing DSST exam score. However, you should keep in mind that not all universities and colleges adhere to the ACE recommendation for DSST credit hours. Some institutions require DSST exam scores higher than the minimum score recommended by ACE. Once you have acquired appropriate reference materials and you have the outline provided on the fact sheet, you are ready to start studying, which is where this book can help.

TEST DAY

After reviewing the material and taking practice tests, you are finally ready to take your DSST exam. Follow these tips for a successful test day experience.

1. **Arrive on time.** Not only is it courteous to arrive on time to the DSST testing facility, but it also allows plenty of time for you to take care of check-in procedures and settle into your surroundings.
2. **Bring identification.** DSST test facilities require that candidates bring a valid government-issued identification card with a current photo and signature. Acceptable forms of identification include a current driver's license, passport, military identification card, or state-issued identification card. Individuals who fail to bring proper identification to the DSST testing facility will not be allowed to take an exam.
3. **Bring the right supplies.** If your exam requires the use of a calculator, you may bring a calculator that meets the specifications. For paper-based exams, you may also bring No. 2 pencils with an eraser and black ballpoint pens. Regardless of the exam methodology, you are NOT allowed to bring reference or study materials, scratch paper, or electronics such as cell phones, personal handheld devices, cameras, alarm wrist watches, or tape recorders to the testing center.
4. **Take the test.** During the exam, take the time to read each question-and-answer option carefully. Eliminate the choices you know are incorrect to narrow the number of potential answers. If a question completely stumps you, take an educated guess and move on—remember that DSSTs are timed; you will have 2 hours to take the exam.

With the proper preparation, DSST exams will save you both time and money. So join the thousands of people who have already reaped the benefits of DSST exams and move closer than ever to your college degree.

FUNDAMENTALS OF COUNSELING EXAM FACTS

The DSST® Fundamentals of Counseling exam consists of 100 multiple-choice questions that assess students for knowledge equivalent to that acquired in a fundamentals of counseling college course. The exam includes the following topics: historical development, counselor roles and functions, the counseling relationship, theoretical approaches, social and cultural foundations, career development, human growth and development, and assessment and appraisal techniques.

Area or Course Equivalent: Fundamentals of Counseling
Level: Lower-level baccalaureate
Amount of Credit: 3 Semester Hours
Minimum Score: 400
Source: www.getcollegecredit.com/wp-content/assets/factsheets/
FundamentalsOfCounseling.pdf

I. **Historical Development – 5%**

   a. Historical events and significant influences

   b. Significant people

II. **Counselor Roles and Functions – 23%**

   a. Counseling as a profession

   b. Role expectations in different counseling settings

   c. Professional associations

   d. Group approaches

   e. Family counseling

   f. Individual counseling

III. **The Counseling Relationship – 12%**

   a. The therapeutic alliance

   b. Counselor characteristics and skills

   c. Ethical and legal issues

IV. **Theoretical Approaches – 24%**

   a. Psychodynamic

   b. Humanistic and experiential

   c. Cognitive–Behavioral

   d. Behavioral

   e. Systems

   f. Postmodern approaches

V. Social and Cultural Foundations – 12%

a. Multicultural Issues (e.g., religion, race, ability, gender and gender identity, sexual orientation, ethnicity, socioeconomics, spiritual, nontraditional approaches, etc.)

b. Discrimination issues (e.g., gender and gender identity, age, sexual orientation, disability, AIDs, managed care, etc.)

c. Societal concerns (e.g., substance abuse, physical and sexual abuse, stress, violence)

VI. Career Development – 6%

a. Theories

b. Decision making models

c. Career information resources

VII. Human Growth and Development – 8%

a. Child development

b. Adolescent development

c. Adulthood

VIII. Assessment and Appraisal Techniques – 10%

a. Testing and measurement

b. Models of assessment

c. Diagnostic and statistical manual for mental disorders (DSM-V)

Chapter 2

Fundamentals of Counseling
Diagnostic Test

DIAGNOSTIC TEST ANSWER SHEET

1. Ⓐ Ⓑ Ⓒ Ⓓ

2. Ⓐ Ⓑ Ⓒ Ⓓ

3. Ⓐ Ⓑ Ⓒ Ⓓ

4. Ⓐ Ⓑ Ⓒ Ⓓ

5. Ⓐ Ⓑ Ⓒ Ⓓ

6. Ⓐ Ⓑ Ⓒ Ⓓ

7. Ⓐ Ⓑ Ⓒ Ⓓ

8. Ⓐ Ⓑ Ⓒ Ⓓ

9. Ⓐ Ⓑ Ⓒ Ⓓ

10. Ⓐ Ⓑ Ⓒ Ⓓ

11. Ⓐ Ⓑ Ⓒ Ⓓ

12. Ⓐ Ⓑ Ⓒ Ⓓ

13. Ⓐ Ⓑ Ⓒ Ⓓ

14. Ⓐ Ⓑ Ⓒ Ⓓ

15. Ⓐ Ⓑ Ⓒ Ⓓ

16. Ⓐ Ⓑ Ⓒ Ⓓ

17. Ⓐ Ⓑ Ⓒ Ⓓ

18. Ⓐ Ⓑ Ⓒ Ⓓ

19. Ⓐ Ⓑ Ⓒ Ⓓ

20. Ⓐ Ⓑ Ⓒ Ⓓ

FUNDAMENTALS OF COUNSELING DIAGNOSTIC TEST
24 minutes—20 questions

Directions: Carefully read each of the following 20 questions. Choose the best answer to each question and fill in the corresponding circle on the answer sheet. The Answer Key and Explanations can be found following this Diagnostic Test.

---

1. After the counseling relationship has ended, counselors should

   A. avoid seeing the client again.
   B. call the client in fixed intervals.
   C. follow up with the client.
   D. call the client infrequently.

2. Narrative therapy and _____ therapy are two post-modern approaches.

   A. Gestalt
   B. cognitive
   C. rational emotive
   D. solution-focused brief

3. Which of the following types of tests measures a range of cognitive abilities and includes tests that measure all of what one has learned?

   A. Aptitude
   B. Diagnostic
   C. Ability
   D. Neuropsychological tests

4. The ACA has _____ sections of its code of ethics.

   A. 9
   B. 8
   C. 7
   D. 6

5. The assessment of _____ includes measuring one's temperament, attitudes, values, likes and dislikes, emotions, motivation, interpersonal skills, and level of adjustment.

   A. behavior
   B. intelligence
   C. personality
   D. aptitude

6. Which law ensures that qualified individuals with disabilities cannot be discriminated against in job application procedures, hiring, firing, advancement, compensation, fringe benefits, and job training, along with other terms, conditions, and privileges?

   A. Americans with Disabilities Act
   B. Carl Perkins Career and Technical Education Act
   C. PL94-142
   D. Rehabilitation Act of 1973

7. _____ developed what some called multigenerational family counseling.

   A. Bowen
   B. Adler
   C. Skinner
   D. Freud

8. Which of the following is an independent organization that develops standards and provides accreditation processes for counseling programs?

   A. CACREP
   B. CORE
   C. ACAF
   D. NBCC

9. The effective counselor needs to be _____ competent in order to connect with his or her clients.

   A. culturally
   B. ethically
   C. legally
   D. psychologically

10. Which type of counseling can be viewed as the development of counselor competencies to maximize effectiveness in their work with all clients?

    A. Individual
    B. Group
    C. Family
    D. Multicultural

11. Which decade saw a large expansion in the use of psychotropic drugs?

    A. 1920s
    B. 1930s
    C. 1940s
    D. 1950s

12. O*NET is an online database developed by the

    A. Department of Statistics.
    B. Department of Labor.
    C. Department of Agriculture.
    D. Department of Justice.

13. Children in which of Piaget's stages are facing a challenge in terms of learning to think abstractly, though they are talented in terms of rational thought?

    A. Sensorimotor
    B. Pre-operational
    C. Concrete-operational
    D. Formal-operational

14. Erikson believed that psychosocial forces combined with _____ and psychological factors to contribute to the development of a healthy person.

    A. biological
    B. emotional
    C. social
    D. spiritual

15. Today, most Gestalt therapists believe that from birth the individual is in a constant state of _____ through a process of need identification and need-fulfillment.

    A. self-regulation
    B. self-actualization
    C. existential crisis
    D. emotional distress

16. Counselors need to have knowledge of how a clients' values, beliefs, and customs will play a part in the counseling relationship, which is related to a client's

    A. cultural background.
    B. psychological history.
    C. clinical diagnoses.
    D. medical/health concerns.

17. Which of the following is another term for positive regard?

    A. Empathy
    B. Genuineness
    C. Acceptance
    D. Active listening

18. Who developed client-centered therapy?

    A. Carl Jung
    B. Viktor Frankl
    C. Carl Rogers
    D. Ludwig Binswanger

19. Which of the following was developed by Albert Ellis during the 1950s?

    A. Psychodynamic therapy
    B. Behavioral therapy
    C. Cognitive therapy
    D. Rational emotive therapy

20. Those who obtain a degree in clinical mental health counseling are generally trained to conduct counseling or psychotherapy for individuals struggling with all of the following EXCEPT:

   A. Life problems
   B. Emotional issues
   C. Mental health issues
   D. Psychotropic medication

ANSWER KEY AND EXPLANATIONS

1. C	5. C	9. A	13. C	17. C
2. D	6. A	10. D	14. A	18. C
3. C	7. A	11. D	15. A	19. D
4. A	8. A	12. B	16. A	20. D

1. **The correct answer is C.** After the counseling relationship has ended, the counselor should follow up with the client. Choice A is incorrect because it may sometimes be necessary for the counselor and client to meet again in the future. Choices B and D are incorrect because there is no single correct way to follow up with a client, and counselors should use their own best judgment of how to do so.

2. **The correct answer is D.** Narrative therapy and solution-focused brief therapy are two post-modern approaches. Gestalt therapy (choice A) is a form of humanistic-existential therapy. Cognitive therapy (choice B) is not a post-modern approach. Rational emotive therapy (choice C) is a form of behavior therapy, which is not a post-modern approach.

3. **The correct answer is C.** Ability tests measure a range of cognitive abilities and include achievement tests, or tests that measure all of what one has learned. Aptitude tests (choice A) measure the likelihood that an individual will do well in a particular area. Diagnostic tests (choice B) are assessments that look for atypical responses, such as a learning disability. Neuropsychological tests (choice D) typically assess cognitive functioning but are not related to achievement tests.

4. **The correct answer is A.** The ACA (American Counseling Association) has nine sections of its code of ethics.

5. **The correct answer is C.** The assessment of personality includes measuring an individual's temperament, attitudes, values, likes and dislikes, emotions, motivation, interpersonal skills, and level of adjustment. Measuring behavior (choice A) would not include gathering information about internal factors like emotions and motivation. Intelligence testing (choice B) does not ask about temperament, attitudes, or values. Aptitude testing (choice D) examines the likelihood that an individual will do well in a particular area based on his or her skills.

6. **The correct answer is A.** The Americans with Disabilities Act ensures that qualified individuals with disabilities cannot be discriminated against in job application procedures, hiring, firing, advancement, compensation, fringe benefits, job training, along with other terms, conditions, and privileges. The Carl Perkins Career and Technical Education Act (choice B) focuses on the academic achievement of career and technical education students. PL94-142 (choice C) maintains access to education for children with a disability. The Rehabilitation Act of 1973 (choice D) prohibits discrimination against individuals with disabilities, but only in federal agencies; it predates the Americans with Disabilities Act.

7. **The correct answer is A.** Bowen developed what some called multigenerational family counseling. Adler (choice B) focused primarily on the influence of birth order in his treatment, but not multigenerational effects. Skinner's treatments (choice C) centered on observable behaviors rather than family influence over time. Finally, while Freud (choice D) was interested in the effects of parenting and childhood experiences, he did not consider how those could transfer from one generation to the next.

8. **The correct answer is A.** CACREP, the Council for Accreditation of Counseling and Related Educational Programs, is an independent organization that develops standards and provides accreditation processes for counseling programs. CORE (choice B) is an acronym for a facilitation technique, not a professional organization. ACAF (choice C) is the foundation that provides grants to American Counseling Association members. Finally, while the NBCC (choice D) is the National Board for Certified Counselors, it provides optional certification rather than program accreditation.

9. **The correct answer is A.** The effective counselor needs to be culturally competent in order to connect with his or her clients. While choices B, C, and D are all important in terms of providing quality care, they are not as vital in terms of making a client connection.

10. **The correct answer is D.** Multicultural counseling can be viewed as the development of counselor competencies to maximize effectiveness in their work with all clients. Individual (choice A), group (choice B), and family (choice C) counseling are more focused and will not affect counselor competency across counseling areas.

11. **The correct answer is D.** The use of psychotropic drugs increased substantially in the 1950s.

12. **The correct answer is B.** O*NET, a listing of available career options, is an online database developed by the Department of Labor.

13. **The correct answer is C.** Children in the concrete-operational stage have not yet developed the capacity to think abstractly, but are good at thinking in logical, rational ways. Children in the sensorimotor stage (choice A) are infants; they are focused on developing object permanence. Children in the pre-operational stage (choice B) are challenged by conservation, or the idea that two objects can look different but consist of the same thing, like a tall, skinny glass of water when compared to a short, fat glass. Adolescents in the formal-operational stage (choice D) have mastered abstract thought.

14. **The correct answer is A.** Erikson believed that psychosocial forces combined with biological and psychological factors to contribute to the development of a healthy person. While emotional (choice B), social (choice C), and spiritual (choice D) factors are important to development, they were not the factors that Erikson focused on.

15. **The correct answer is A.** Today, most Gestalt therapists believe that starting at birth, the individual is in a constant state of self-regulation through a process of need identification and need fulfillment. Self-actualization (choice B) is the process of growing into the best version of oneself through striving to reach goals. An existential crisis (choice C) is when an individual questions if their life has meaning, and typically happens in a short time frame, rather than from birth. Emotional distress (choice D) is often similarly short-lived and has little to do with the identification of needs.

16. **The correct answer is A.** Counselors need to have knowledge of the cultural background of the client, which includes how a clients' values, beliefs, and customs will play a part in the counseling relationship. Psychological history (choice B), clinical diagnoses (choice C), and medical/health concerns (choice D) are unrelated to the customs, values, and beliefs of the client and how they will play a part in the counseling relationship.

17. **The correct answer is C.** Acceptance is another term for unconditional positive regard. Empathy (choice A) is more accurately thought of as being able to see the world from another person's viewpoint. Genuineness (choice B) refers to honesty during interactions with a client. Active listening (choice D) involves focusing on what a client is saying, asking questions, and nodding to provide encouragement to keep speaking, among other things.

18. **The correct answer is C.** Carl Rogers developed client-centered therapy. Carl Jung (choice A) was a psychoanalyst and did not agree with the guidelines to client-centered therapy. Viktor Frankl (choice B) is associated with logotherapy rather than client-centered therapy. Ludwig Binswanger (choice D) was a pioneer in existential psychology and did not focus on therapy.

19. **The correct answer is D.** Albert Ellis developed rational emotive behavior therapy in the 1950s. Sigmund Freud would be accurately associated with psychodynamic therapy (choice A). While rational emotive therapy is a form of behavior therapy, choice B is incorrect because behavioral therapy itself is more commonly linked with B.F. Skinner. Cognitive therapy (choice C) was initially created by Aaron Beck.

20. **The correct answer is D.** Individuals who earn a degree in clinical mental health counseling generally work with individuals struggling with life problems, emotional issues, and mental health issues. They are not, however, trained to work with those struggling with medication; for that, clients should see a psychiatrist or perhaps another medical doctor.

DIAGNOSTIC TEST ASSESSMENT GRID

Now that you've completed the diagnostic test and read through the answer explanations, you can use your results to target your studying. Find the question numbers from the diagnostic test that you answered incorrectly and highlight or circle them below. Then focus extra attention on the sections dealing with those topics.

Fundamentals of Counseling		
Content Area	**Topic**	**Question #**
Historical Development	• Historical events and significant influences • Significant people	11
Counselor Roles and Functions	• Counseling as a profession • Role expectations in different counseling settings • Professional associations • Group approaches • Family counseling • Individual counseling	1, 7, 8, 16, 19
The Counseling Relationship	• The therapeutic alliance • Counselor characteristics and skills • Ethical and legal issues	4, 9, 17
Theoretical Approaches	• Psychodynamic • Humanistic and experiential • Cognitive–Behavioral • Behavioral • Systems • Postmodern approaches	2, 15, 18, 20
Social and Cultural Foundations	• Multicultural issues • Discrimination issues • Societal concerns	6, 10
Career Development	• Theories • Decision making models • Career information resources	12

Fundamentals of Counseling

Content Area	Topic	Question #
Human Growth and Development	• Child development • Adolescent development • Adulthood	13, 14
Assessment and Appraisal Techniques	• Testing and measurement • Models of assessment • Diagnostic and statistical manual for mental disorders (DSM-V)	3, 5

Chapter 3

Fundamentals of Counseling Subject Review

OVERVIEW
- **Historical Development**
- **Counselor Roles and Functions**
- **The Counseling Relationship**
- **Theoretical Approaches**
- **Social and Cultural Foundations**
- **Career Development**
- **Human Growth and Development**
- **Assessment and Appraisal Techniques**
- **Summing It Up**

HISTORICAL DEVELOPMENT

It's important to begin by talking about history, and specifically, how historical events have influenced the direction of the field of counseling. We know that helping behavior is not new—in fact, "helping" in prehistoric times can be seen as a precursor to human services work today.

Historical Events and Significant Influences

Back when humans were living in caves, most human problems were attributed to evil spirits or demons. The helpers assisted by exorcising these spirits, promoting wellness. Later, early civilizations like Ancient Greece and Rome started examining human behavior through empirical study. Any sort of psychological problems or deviant behavior could be viewed as having organic causes. This is similar to medicine, where sickness is viewed as being caused by something physical happening in the body. This meant that helpers used treatments that we may think of as medical, like leeches to suck out "bad blood." While there were individuals trying to help those suffering, there was also a lack of services, and in some cases, unnecessarily cruel treatments were used.

In the Middle Ages, Christianity became a dominant world power. This led to the Church developing and providing a variety of human services. Monasteries often served as both sanctuaries and places of treatment for the mentally ill. The Church also created institutions for the poor and people with disabilities, and sponsored orphanages and homes for the elderly. While early on these services were housed within church facilities, ultimately, they were moved to nonreligious sites.

During the Renaissance, the responsibility to provide physical and mental health services was moved to the state itself. Over time, this led to conflict, as both parties debated who could, and should, provide services. Ultimately, as the state took over, there were some negative results, particularly because the state tended to prioritize those it saw as "deserving" of help. This led to the rise of healthcare inequality.

In 1601, the **Elizabethan Poor Law** established a system in England that provided care for the poor, including shelter. Additionally, it specified the chain of responsibility for the poor and disadvantaged. First and foremost, it was the responsibility of the family to provide for all human services. If the family could not provide such services, it then became the state's job to do so. As a result of the Poor Laws in England, a system for classifying the disadvantaged into three categories was established:

1. the poor who were capable of work
2. the poor who were incapable of work because of age, physical disability, or motherhood responsibilities
3. orphaned or abandoned children who became wards of the state

With that, human services became more and more organized. Additional policies were created to decide who was eligible for available services and who made that decision. As the Industrial Revolution moved people into cities, human services became centralized, and more people were fighting for fewer services. Some at this time advocated for **social Darwinism**, or very simply put, the idea that disadvantaged people should not be helped and should be left to die.

In terms of mental health resources specifically, early public mental institutions in Europe and the United States were located within communities, and the communities were responsible for their maintenance and functioning. There were no universal guidelines for procedures or patient care, and unfortunately, abuse and other forms of mistreatment were common.

A backlash to these issues spawned early reform movements in the United States. This led to more professionalized services and increased opportunities to help. During the late 1770s and early 1780s, a reform movement began that would alter significantly, although briefly, the existing conditions in mental institutions. This movement has been referred to as the **era of humanitarian reform** and the **moral treatment movement**. In particular, **Dorothea Dix** was instrumental in gathering enough public support to make greatly needed changes to the inhumane conditions of the asylums, along with prisons and shelters for the poor.

During WWI, the first tests of achievement were used on men entering the war. These tests were administered to the soldiers to discover where they would be the most useful. This is also when the first cases of what we now know as Post-Traumatic Stress Disorder were recognized and treatment was attempted. By the 1920s and 1930s, **Sigmund Freud's** classic theories concerning human behavior were widely accepted. These impacted the prevailing treatment approach, and most mental institutions of the time became psychoanalytically oriented (we will discuss this concept later in this chapter).

In the early 1950s, the growth of psychopharmacology brought about more changes in the field, as medication was used to control patient behavior, leading to opportunities for treatment. The use of psychotropic drugs increased substantially in this decade. Some critics claimed that patients were controlled unnecessarily, as they were routinely given unneeded drugs; others grew concerned that the side effects of some medications could be devastating.

Also during the 1940s and 1950s, there was an increased emphasis on the understanding between different types of systems and how they interacted, including social and family systems. This led to the development of systems theory, which we will discussed more later. Vocational guidance was first used in schools before it grew into a separate field of specialization.

Around the same time, **deinstitutionalization** became a major policy. There was a growing belief that people could be treated more successfully in familiar community settings, leading to what some call the third mental health revolution in the 1960s. Since then, the role of the generalist human services worker, has grown to include a wide range of therapeutic activities.

At this point in time, new methods and approaches are still needed to deal with both mental and physical health in our complex world. In order to stay relevant, the human services system, including counseling, must grow and change with the times.

Significant People

There have been many individuals that have influenced the field of counseling throughout its development. This section provides an introductory review of key significant people. Specific details regarding key players in the field are discussed throughout this chapter.

Early on, **John Dewey** was a large influence through his writings in education, which affected the work of other helping professionals. Later, some social workers who assisted the poor were equally vital to the field, including **Jesse Davis**, **Anna Reed**, and **Eli Weaver**. The idea of counseling as a form of vocational guidance was largely influenced by **Frank Parsons** (sometimes called the "founder" of guidance in America) and **Jane Addams**.

Another significant influence was the spread of psychotherapy in the realm of psychology, which occurred from 1900–1950. Initially, **Clifford Beers** and his book *A Mind that Found Itself* made an impact. Later, **E.G. Williamson's** Minnesota Point of View (a trait and factor theory) had an influence in the field, as did **Carl Rogers** and his Rochester Guidance Clinic. All of these led to an increased spread of the field of counseling, as counselors moved from schools into other areas.

Along with this increased diversification in the 1960s, professionals like **Albert Ellis**, **Albert Bandura**, **Joseph Wolpe**, and **John Krumboltz** influenced counseling through their commitment to different schools of theory and therapy, specifically the influence of behaviorism. **Fritz Perls** pushed Gestalt therapy, and **Viktor Frankl** and **Rollo May** were invested in existential therapy. The most famous cognitive therapist is likely **Aaron Beck**, though Alfred Adler also played a role in this field. In terms of psychoanalytic methods, you've already read about Sigmund Freud; **Carl Jung** is extremely important as well.

Later, others pushed for the development of multicultural counseling, including **Derald Wing Sue**, **Paul Pedersen**, and **Donald Atkinson**.

While this is only a subset of the individuals that influenced the development of counseling as a field, these are the key names that you should be familiar with, as these individuals had a major influence in the foundation and growth of the field.

COUNSELOR ROLES AND FUNCTIONS

Counselors are trained to offer support and advice to individuals and groups who are seeking help in a variety of areas, including alcohol and drug addiction, child abuse, or reaching career and academic objectives. They also help clients seeking advice regarding marital, family, and spiritual issues. Unlike psychologists, most counselors place little, if any, emphasis on long-term analysis and psychodynamics. Instead, they prefer to offer possible alternatives and solutions to specific problems of daily living. Individuals who go into counseling typically obtain a master's degree in their field, and some states require additional licensure above that. Licensure is the most rigorous form of credentialing. The most common area in which to earn a degree is clinical mental health counseling.

While there are many areas of counseling, counselors should only practice in an area for which they have undergone training. It's also important that they use theories based on sound scientific evidence (more on theories will be discussed later). Counselors should obtain supervision throughout their training process, as it will allow them to practice at optimal levels. The daily roles of a counselor will differ depending on where the individual is practicing. For instance, one of the major roles of school psychologists is to test children within the school system, whether for learning disabilities or aptitude for a specialized program. In contrast, a substance use counselor may do little testing.

While there are some differences in role expectations in varied settings, generally, counselors are responsible for working effectively with all of their clients. In addition, counselors have a **duty to warn**—if they feel that a client is a possible danger from self-harm or harm to others, they are required to report the information to the proper authorities. This is one time when **confidentiality** between a counselor and patient can be broken. Not all therapists have **privileged communication** but those who do have a right to withhold information about their clients, as that information is protected. Counselors also need to have knowledge of the cultural background of the client and how the clients' values, beliefs, and customs will play a part in the counseling relationship.

Professional Associations

There are a multitude of professional associations for counselors. Some benefits of a professional association include the ability to attend national and regional conferences to learn more about developments in the field and network with other professionals in your specific area, plus access to newsletters, blogs, job banks, and mentoring opportunities. There are often lobbyists that work with professional associations to help get causes, that are important to their members, in front of government officials.

Additionally, membership in a professional organization typically gives members access to malpractice insurance, which will protect counselors in the event there is an incident with a client in their care. The organizations typically provide their own codes of ethics and standards for practice, which can be valuable reference materials.

The largest counseling-specific professional association is the **American Counseling Association (ACA)**. There are 18 chartered divisions and many other related associations, including the **American Counseling Association Foundation (ACAF)**, the **Council on Rehabilitation Education (CORE)**, the **National Board for Certified Counselors (NBCC)**, and **Chi Sigma Iota (CSI)**. There are 56 branches of ACA, including 50 state branches, Puerto Rico, Washington D.C., and associations in Latin America and Europe. There are also four regional associations in the United States. The **Council for Accreditation of Counseling and Related Educational Programs (CACREP)** is also important; it's an independent organization that develops standards and provides accreditation processes for counseling programs.

In addition, the following are some other associations that are popular amongst counselors:
- American Art Therapy Association (AATA)
- American Association for Marriage and Family Therapy (AAMFT)
- American Psychiatric Association (APA)
- American Psychiatric Nurses Association (APNA)
- American Psychological Association (APA)
- National Association of Social Workers (NASW)
- National Organization for Human Services (NOHS)

Group Approaches

Group counseling has become much more popular over the years due in part to the dynamic interactions between members. In this environment, counselors can observe communication patterns, power dynamics, hierarchies, and even homeostasis.

Prior to 1900, individuals were placed into functional, pragmatic groups to work on things like daily living skills. These groups were often moralistic—others outside the group decided what the patients "needed." Later, Jane Addams and Mary Richmond used community groups as a way to make systemic changes.

Around the turn of the century, vocation and moral guidance were being covered in schools. Dr. Henry Pratt, a physician, was meeting with tuberculosis patients in groups and having them tell their own stories—much like the support groups that we see today.

Also around 1900, psychoanalytic principles were often used to explain group behavior. Primal urges and instincts were discussed, along with the influence of parents. Group behavior was examined in terms of how things start to go wrong, something termed **mob behavior** at the time. In 1914, the phrase **group psychotherapy** was coined.

In the 1920s and 1930s, Alfred Adler's influence was strongly felt, as researchers and counselors alike began to examine the effects of birth order and social connectedness. These were the first non-psychoanalytically oriented groups. More group guidance was also happening in the school system during this time period.

The emergence of modern-day groups occurred in the 1940s when Carl Rogers worked with soldiers returning after WWII, and others were leading similar groups around different issues. By the 1960s, it was thought that groups were ideal therapy, representing freedom and love. Group therapy's popularity increased substantially, and throughout the 1960s and 1970s, books on group counseling also increased. The American Psychological Association published the "Guidelines for Psychologists Conducting Growth Groups" in 1973.

As groups became a popular alternative to individual counseling common-theme, task groups, and time-limited or brief groups became common. This period saw a rise in **self-help groups**. The purpose of self-help groups is both educational and affirmational, with the overall goal being to enhance members' strengths. The groups usually focus on specific issues, like alcohol abuse or eating disorders. There is typically not a paid leader, and a nominal fee is charged.

Task groups are another popular type of group. These groups focus on conscious behaviors and group dynamics. Specialists typically enter a system and help to diagnose and analyze problems. Often, they focus on differences between people and how to get along.

Psychoeducational groups, once called "guidance groups," focus on disseminating mental health education, and ultimately empowering members individually and as a unit. This type of group is found in many settings and typically has a designated, well-trained group leader. Essentially, these groups focus on preventative education.

A **counseling group** often focuses on prevention along with general wellness, insight, and self-actualization, or on members becoming the best possible version of themselves.

At this point, almost all education options for counselors include time spent on group work and the dynamics and processes of groups. Counselors are not usually dealing with severe issues; rather, they are focused on issues related to typical human development. Groups often have 4-12 members and a well-trained leader.

In true **group therapy**, the focus is on deep-seated, long-term issues. The leader is well trained, and the group is similar in size to a counseling group. The goal is the remediation of severe pathology and personality reconstruction. The therapy group usually meets for a minimum of eight sessions, at least once a week, for 1–3 hours at a time.

When related to group counseling, theory gives the counselor a comprehensive system to use as a framework, which allows counselors to understand their clients better and helps them decide which techniques to apply. Theory is also useful in predicting the course of treatment, and it is researchable, which allows the gathering of information about the efficacy of a specific treatment method. Most theories can be applied to group work, and theories that have been successfully applied include psychoanalytic, existential-humanistic, cognitive-behavioral, and post-modern.

If a counselor decides to try to start a form of group work, it's important to think about several factors.

- Where will members come from?
- Should the group composition be varied or homogeneous?
- Will the group be a closed group where new members are not admitted or open to new faces at any point?
- How long should meetings last?
- How often should the meetings take place?
- Where will the group meet?

Group work is divided into a few stages. In the **pregroup stage**, the group is forming. A pregroup meeting is set and potential members can be interviewed to identify expectations and challenge any myths. At this point, members can be screened out or accepted into the group. Members should also sign an informed consent document agreeing to participate and to any group rules. In the **initial stage**, the group is meeting but still forming. Members are often anxious to get started and tend to focus on others rather than themselves. The group leader defines ground rules and builds trust. Structure, empathy, and positive regard are all important in this stage.

In the **transition stage**, members are becoming more comfortable, often positioning themselves into their own subgroups. They understand the ground rules and any technical issues. Members may project their feelings onto the group leader and may attack other members during group discussions. As this stage continues, though, trust slowly builds, and resistance diminishes. Ultimately, members identify their problems and goals, and begin to identify their own feelings.

In the **word stage**, trust occurs, conflict lessens, and overall group cohesion occurs. Group members can both give and receive feedback and can work on identified behavioral change. Members report gains in self-esteem as well. For leaders, this is when the use of advanced counseling skills takes place.

As groups end, they enter the **closure stage**. Group members report an increased sense of accomplishment and will share what they've learned and also express feelings about other group members. The leader should summarize using empathy and consider who may want to follow-up with further counseling. At the end, everyone says goodbye.

It's important to remember that groups can be influenced by culture in both positive and negative ways. Groups can help any "privileged" clients to see their privilege but can also mimic what happens in society in a negative way. If the group leader is of a different culture than the group members, the members may project feelings about the leader's culture onto the leader. This offers the leader opportunity to have clients understand their biases.

In terms of ethics, the biggest issue is confidentiality. How can the counselor ensure confidentiality? While it's important to keep this at the forefront, this is something that the informed consent form can specifically address.

Family Counseling

Let's move to a discussion of family counseling, starting with a brief history. Family counseling's roots can be traced to the 1800s, when Charity Organization Societies and "friendly visitors" worked with poor families, trying to provide support. Until the 1940s, families were generally not seen together due to pressure placed on therapist from the developing "individual approaches" to counseling. Around the 1950s, a number of treatment approaches developed, and many approaches started to include families. Here's a brief list of treatment options specifically related to families, some which will be discussed in more detail later:

- **Satir:** Human validation process model
- **Haley and Madanes:** Strategic therapy
- **Whitaker:** Experiential approach
- **Minuchin:** Structural family therapy
- **1966:** Brief Family Therapy Center
- **1970s:** Milan Group
- **More recently:** Narrative family therapy (White and Epston)

Today, every state in the United States has marriage and family counseling licensure options. The two main associations are the American Association for Marriage and Family Therapy (AAMFT) and the International Association of Marriage and Family Counselors (IAMFC), which is a division of ACA. There are also two main accreditation bodies: the Commission on Accreditation for Marriage and Family Therapy Education (COAMFTE) and the Council for Accreditation of Counseling and Related Educational Programs (CACREP). The efficacy of family treatment has been shown through research. The following paragraphs will highlight a few theories used to explain the success of family treatment.

In **general systems theory**, the interaction of all types of systems is thought to affect the other systems. A healthy system has semi-permeable boundaries; unhealthy systems have either rigid or diffuse boundaries. According to this theory, American culture allows for much variability in boundaries, which can be a problem. In addition, there are rules for the hierarchy within systems—both universal rules that are easily understood and idiosyncratic rules that are harder to follow. Rules can be either overt or covert, and they're often related to the hierarchical structure.

Another theory related to family counseling is **communication theory**. The general idea is that all couples bring unfinished business to a relationship, and this unfinished business can lead to discontent, as couples blame each other for their projected problems. In families, members may focus on one member in particular, rather than their individual problems. Families sometimes enter counseling because they bring in the "scapegoat," or initial client, and say that the client has a problem. When family members are unhappy with each other and either directly or indirectly take it out on a specific family member, that family member has been scapegoated.

A common issue discussed in family counseling is stress and its effects. This can happen due to the stressful contact of one member with extra-familial forces (e.g., difficulty at work). It can also occur because of the stressful contact of the whole family with extra-familial forces (e.g., a natural disaster such as a hurricane). Stress can happen at transitional or developmental points in the family (e.g., puberty, midlife crises, retirement, aging). There can also be idiosyncratic (or situational) stress, like an unexpected illness.

Social constructionism believes that some other theories place too much emphasis on causal factors. Social constructionists believe that couples and families "co-construct" their understanding of who they are through ongoing dialogue and nonverbal interactions among people in the couple or family and the broader culture. In this theory, change occurs through conversations with the counselor. Together, the counselor and the clients construct a new system.

The **human validation process model** was created by Virginia Satir, a prominent humanist of the twentieth century. According to this theory, there are four universal communication patterns (placater, blamer, computer, and distracter), and congruent, respectful, and caring parents yield healthy children. Two well-known techniques of this model are to complete a family life facto chronology and to use family sculpting.

In **structural family therapy**, Salvadore Minuchin came up with interactional and transactional rules that govern family groups that are related to the structure and hierarchy of the family. There are some common techniques that can be used, including joining, mapping, and restructuring. This type of therapy is focused on changing communication sequences—there is no focus on feelings, except to help people feel better. The main concern is how power is dispersed in families.

Another popular option is **multigenerational family therapy**, which is usually attributed to Murray Bowen. This model assumes that ways of relating within a family are passed down, including loyalties, indebtedness, and entitlements. Families need to work on this system in therapy to move past it.

It's also important to discuss **psychodynamic family therapy**, attributed primarily to Robin Skynner and Nathan Ackerman. The emphasis here is how parents assist children through the developmental stages. In this theory, the problems in each parent are thought to be reflected through the unconscious, and these unfinished problems are projected onto the family. The couple explores how behaviors are related to their own childhoods in therapy.

In **cognitive-behavioral family counseling**, the treatment is focused on symptom relief. It is highly structured and focuses on behaviors and cognitions, pulling from operant conditioning, classical conditioning, and modeling, or social learning theory. In essence, this type of treatment focuses on changing automatic negative thoughts and the behaviors that they cause. Additionally, it integrates how problems get infused in a family through the system.

In **narrative family therapy**, usually attributed to Michael White and David Epston, the goal is to recreate how the family comes to understand itself. Family members deconstruct the past narrative and construct new narratives that are healthier and more functional.

Another popular approach, **solution-focused family therapy**, is pragmatic and future-oriented. This approach assumes that clients can change quickly, and it focuses on solutions and the use of problem-free language to discuss the family structure.

Regardless of the specific type of family counseling, all counselors should consider or be aware of the following:

- Counselors need a multicultural and social justice focus, particularly when working with minority families.
- The use of the word "marriage" can be problematic. The traditional definition may not apply in certain situations as there are many individuals in long-term partnerships that cannot or choose not to get married for a variety of reasons.
- In terms of ethics, it's important to avoid withholding treatment from an individual in order to see the "whole" family first.
- Obtain informed consent for everyone in treatment.
- It's difficult to guarantee confidentiality for everyone involved. It's important to know the law in any given state as far as child, spousal, and family abuse, and the rules about custody.
- Family therapists can also get in trouble for insurance fraud by saying that they're seeing "one" member in the family when they are actually seeing the entire family.
- Lastly, there are some problems with multiple relationships. Should a counselor be seeing a member individually and also as part of a family? Many researchers say no, as it's hard to maintain impartiality in those cases.

Individual Counseling

Let's move forward to a discussion of individual counseling. Some view this type of treatment as an opportunity to receive support and experience growth during challenging times in life. It can help people deal with personal topics ranging from emotional problems to school difficulties, career changes, and more. Individual counseling is sometimes referred to as psychotherapy, talk therapy, or treatment. All these terms serve to describe a situation where a patient sees a trained counselor on a one-on-one basis in a safe and caring environment. Individual counseling allows individuals to explore their feelings, beliefs, and behaviors; identify aspects of their lives that they would like to change; better understand themselves and others; set personal goals; and/or work toward desired change.

Typically, this type of counseling focuses on immediate or near future concerns. Common reasons that a person will seek this type of treatment include problems at work, dealing with the death of a loved one, or trouble adjusting after a move or a breakup. Generally, the goal is to help clients heal, grow, and move forward to a psychologically healthy life.

Research has shown that individual counseling results in fewer relapses of common conditions like moderate depression and anxiety, and that the positive effects of good therapy extend well beyond treatment. In fact, many clients report improved conditions long after therapy has ended. In general, counseling is often more effective than psychotropic drugs or medical treatments alone.

THE COUNSELING RELATIONSHIP

The **therapeutic alliance** (sometimes called the helping alliance or the working alliance) refers to the relationship between a healthcare professional and a client (or patient). It is the means by which a therapist and a client hope to engage with each other and bring about beneficial change in the client. In other words, this is the bond felt between the therapist and the client, and it is the most powerful factor in the process of healing through counseling.

Hundreds of studies indicate that a strong, purposeful, collaborative relationship between the counselor and the client is positively correlated with treatment progress. This is because treatment requires that the counselor and the client work together, and that the client trust the counselor in order to make change. The most effective counselors are those who focus specifically on building the therapeutic alliance.

Counselor Characteristics and Skills

There are certain counselor characteristics and skills that are commonly related to successful treatment and to the formation of the therapeutic alliance. The first of these is **empathy**, or the ability to take the viewpoint of others and understand how they are feeling in a given situation. More than anything else, this trait is related to positive outcomes for clients in treatment. While this is a personal characteristic, it's also a skill that can be learned, and is encouraged in the schooling process for counselors.

Related to this is **acceptance**, which is sometimes referred to as positive regard. With acceptance, the counselor views the client with respect regardless of what the client says or does. This is a required foundation for the therapeutic alliance—it is directly related to the formation of trust. For the counselor, acceptance is the suspension of judgment. Counselors must accept their clients without any strings attached. Regardless of the specific treatment type, almost all counseling approaches emphasize acceptance of the client and the client acceptance of self.

Another important characteristic is **genuineness**, which refers to the willingness of the therapist to be authentic, open, and honest within the helping relationship. Research on genuineness shows that it may be important in client outcomes and related to emotional intelligence, which is the ability to monitor one's emotions. This is important because counseling relationships are related to the actual relationship between the client and the counselor—without being genuine, it is difficult to form that relationship.

It is important that counselors embrace a **wellness** perspective. Counselors can easily become stressed, burned out, have compassion fatigue, and experience vicarious traumatization—all which can lead to **countertransference**, or the counselor accidentally taking things out on the client. Counselors are encouraged to take care of themselves and their health, and perhaps seek out treatment of their own.

Counselors must have some level of **cultural competence**. Clients from nondominant groups are sometimes distrustful of counselors. They are often misunderstood and misdiagnosed, find counseling unhelpful, attend counseling less frequently, and drop out more quickly. Culture influences all relationships, but it is especially important for helping professionals like counselors to be sensitive to the experiences of others.

Counselors also need to find a theory that "fits" their client's individual personality and style. The more a client feels comfortable and understands a theory, the more the client will believe in it. Strong belief in a theory helps clients to trust in the helper's approach, thus yielding better client outcomes overall. Related to this, counselor expertise has been shown to be crucial for client success in counseling. The counselor's desire to join professional associations, mentor and supervise others, read professional journals, take continuing education classes, and keep broadening their approach are all viewed as positive, valuable things by their clients. This is why the ACA encourages counselors to practice only within the area in which they're trained and certified.

Ethical and Legal Issues

As mentioned previously, there are ethical and legal issues specifically related to counseling. Counselors need to focus on confidentiality outside of very specific situations where it is waived either for legal reasons or out of concern for the safety of others. While specific laws differ from state to state, counselors are generally mandated reporters and need to report suspected abuse to the proper authorities. Some more specific examples will be discussed later in this chapter. The ACA has nine sections in its code of ethics that cover a range of situations. Distance Counseling, Technology, and Social Media is the section most recently added to the ACA Code of Ethics, in 2014.

There are a few laws and rulings that we will mention here. The federal law that ensures parents the right to access their children's educational records, though counseling notes are generally excluded, is the **Federal Education Rights and Privacy Act (FERPA)**. The ruling in *Jaffee v. Redmond* is related to the confidentiality of the client and therapist relationship. *Tarasoff v. Regents of University of California* is the ruling that established duty to warn, which was mentioned earlier. *Julea Ward v. Board of Regents of Eastern Michigan University* is related to ethics in counseling; specifically, to the need to follow the ACA ethical code when providing treatment, regardless of one's personal beliefs.

In addition, it's important for counselors to keep tabs on their own mental and physical health, and to seek treatment as needed. Counselors have a responsibility to know when an impairment will negatively affect their clients, and when to limit or terminate work if needed. This is because impairment can lead to incompetence, which is unethical, can be illegal, and could lead to malpractice suits.

THEORETICAL APPROACHES

Theory gives counselors a framework in which to work, allowing them to make decisions and suggestions with a strong basis. There are quite a few theories related to counseling, and it's important to keep in mind that there is not one theory that is truly "best." In short, the best theory is one that is carefully applied to a specific problem and treatment option.

Psychodynamic

Let's begin with a discussion of the psychodynamic theory and viewpoint. The development of psychoanalysis is very much associated with **Sigmund Freud** and his followers. **Psychoanalysis** is based upon the idea that individuals are often unaware of what underlies his or her emotions and behavior. These "unconscious" factors may contribute to difficulties, leading to the development of symptoms like anxiety, depression, or problems in interpersonal relationships. The **id** (unconscious part of the mind), **ego** (moderator concerned with reality), and **superego** (conscience or moral guideline) are in constant conflict, and free association—where the client talks without any clear path, simply jumping from thought to thought at will—can be used to identify these conflicts. True psychoanalysis was very popular during the 1930s and 1940s, but with the rise of behaviorism, its popularity lessened. Even so, some psychodynamic concepts are still used commonly today.

The therapist who practices classical psychoanalysis seeks to maintain a sense of neutrality and objectivity with the client—there is very little self-disclosure by the therapist. This is considered essential to the method, but it goes against much of the research on the therapeutic alliance mentioned previously. Even so, this was the first comprehensive approach to therapy.

One common element still used today is that early childhood has some long-term effects on the development of personality and on challenges that individuals face. According to this theory, one's past, in interaction with the conscious and unconscious, affects a person's development. Parenting affects development specifically through stages, which Freud called the psychosexual stages of development, and defense mechanisms kick in and reflect that development. Overall, this type of treatment relies on making the unconscious conscious, using techniques like free association, the analysis of dreams, and the development of a transference relationship. With **transference**, the client projects his or her unconscious memories of previous problematic relationships (often with a parent) onto his or her relationship with the counselor, changing the relationship and allowing it to be analyzed and ultimately dealt with in a positive way.

Analytic or **Jungian Therapy**, developed by **Carl Jung**, spun off from traditional Freudian psychoanalysis. Jung was less pessimistic than Freud and was interested in personality types and how individuals function. He believed that information that matches psychological type goes into the **consciousness**; information that doesn't match goes into the **personal unconscious**. Jung also posited that humans have a **collective unconscious**, which is inherited, and is related to the tendency to perceive things in ways that we call human. Jung believed that humans could make almost anything unconscious, and that if an individual understands his or her personal and collective unconscious, that individual is "whole." Due to this, the goal of techniques with this type of treatment is to make the unconscious conscious by examining dreams and the meaning of symbols, along with creative techniques and the use of an active imagination. Jung also believed that each individual has a unique psychological type that includes the characteristics of extraversion and introversion.

Another offshoot of psychoanalysis, **individual psychology**, is also referred to as **Adlerian Therapy** because it was developed by Alfred Adler. He believed in **teleology**, the idea that we as humans are inherently goal directed and strive to fulfill one drive—perfection. Because we inevitably fall short, we feel inferior, and this is simply a part of being human. The drive toward our subjective goal results in development of behaviors that compensate for feelings of inferiority. Adler believed that you could tell how a person is driven toward his or her goal through his or her **style of life**. This is sometimes seen as an early humanistic approach, as it suggests that through education and counseling, one can change. He also believed that every child was born with innate and unique capabilities and is inherently moving toward the future, not determined by the past.

This was one of the first approaches to working with families. Techniques include exploring the family constellation (or how a family is made up), examining early memories, encouragement, discussion groups, setting limits, and acting "as if" something is already true. Adlerian therapists also use simple and logical thoughts to communicate with their clients.

Humanistic and Experiential

The humanistic and experiential theory is loosely based on existential philosophy. It deals with the struggles of living and how humans construct meaning in their lives. This type of treatment tends to be optimistic, and focuses on consciousness, relationships, and helping people "self-actualize," or become the best possible versions of themselves.

The humanistic perspective emphasizes the unique qualities of humans, especially their capacity for choice and their potential for personal growth. The humanistic approach is based on the concept of **self-actualization**, or the tendency for humans to be motivated to develop to full capacity. People seeking humanistic therapy want to take responsibility for their own happiness and develop a more positive self-concept. Some critics believe that humanists exaggerate the benefits of the therapist's accepting attitude during therapy. It may take more than an attitude of positive regard to transform the client into a self-actualizing person. Even so, this perspective connects well with how many counselors see the helping relationship.

Humanistic therapists practice a client-centered approach in which the therapist does not actively establish goals or provide specific advice or direction to the client. The basic premise is that clients are capable of self-directed growth and have a great potential for resolving their own problems if provided with a helping relationship that facilitates such growth. There are three main approaches: existential therapy, person-centered therapy, and Gestalt therapy.

The central tenets of most existential approaches include that humans are born into a world with no inherent meaning, so we make our own meaning. This means that we struggle throughout our lives to be "human." We have a choice about who we are, and we can choose to examine our choices and learn about ourselves.

In **person-centered counseling** (also called **client-centered therapy**), developed by **Carl Rogers**, the main focus is that humans all have a need to be regarded with respect. We also have conditions of worth, or guidelines for what we need to do to be loved, placed on by our significant others. Therapists in this area help people become more congruent, or realistic, about the kind of person that they are, and also help clients to gain a more realistic sense of their ideal self. Techniques used in this type of therapy include those mentioned earlier in the chapter: unconditional positive regard, empathy, and genuineness.

With **Gestalt Therapy**, developed by **Fritz Perls**, the client is only aware of his or her own needs in the "foreground." This leads to unfinished business, as needs never make their way to the forefront and therefore are not met. This type of therapy is more directive and confrontational, and techniques push the client into experiencing the now. Today, most Gestalt therapists believe that starting at birth, the individual is in a constant state of self-regulation through need identification and need fulfillment. One particular method of Gestalt therapy technique encourages clients to take ownership of their defensive projections with the use of "I" statements, which allows them to continue self-regulation.

Cognitive–Behavioral

The cognitive-behavioral approaches are largely based on major areas in the behaviorist school of thought, including classical conditioning, operant conditioning, and modeling or social learning theory. In recent years, an added focus has been based on cognitive structures and the elimination of illogical ways of thinking.

In **cognitive therapy (CBT)**, the counselor and the client focus on problem areas and set goals. The counselor then chooses the techniques that will work best to attain those goals, and ultimately assesses goal completion before ending therapy. CBT does not deal with the underlying issues; rather, it focuses on solving the problems that are caused by these underlying thoughts. There are a few common types of therapy in this area, including rational emotive behavior therapy, cognitive therapy, reality therapy, and choice theory.

In **rational emotive behavior therapy (REBT)**, developed by **Albert Ellis**, there is a complex interaction between thinking, feeling, and acting. The main focus is rational versus irrational thinking, and on fixing an individual's cognitive distortions. In this type of therapy, the relationship is important but not critical.

In **cognitive therapy**, pioneered by **Aaron Beck**, the effects of previous cognitive distortions are thought to continue into the present day. In addition, the addition of stress is thought to be related to the development of our unique disorders. This type of therapy is rational, pragmatic, antideterministic, educative, and empirical. According to this school of thought, humans all have "core beliefs" that drive us—embedded beliefs are often out of our awareness, and these beliefs can be negative. These core beliefs lead to intermediate beliefs (attitudes, rules, and expectations), that lead to automatic thoughts. Automatic thoughts are related to certain cognitive distortions, which can lead to reactions to certain situations. In treatment, the focus is on automatic thoughts, to get to intermediate beliefs, then get to core beliefs—change core beliefs through thinking and acting differently.

In **reality therapy/choice theory**, humans are thought to have five genetically based needs: survival, love and belonging, power, freedom, and fun. Each person has a unique "need-strength profile," and we can only satisfy our needs and control our behaviors in the present. Since birth, we as humans create a "quality world" to determine how to satisfy our needs, but some quality worlds lead to destructive behaviors. We can change the pictures in our quality worlds and our behaviors, and therapy helps with this.

Behavioral

While CBT does include a focus on behavior as well as cognition, it's also true that there's a behavioral model of counseling that treats only observable behavior. The early behaviorists believed that important laws governing behavior could be revealed by studying the behavior of animals—cats, dogs, rats, pigeons—in carefully controlled experimental situations. The emphasis was on conditioning, which involved situations that brought about a change in the behavior of the organism. Two general kinds of conditioning were identified and designated as classical and operant conditioning, as already mentioned.

John B. Watson helped to introduce behaviorism to the general public. His classic study with a white rat and Little Albert showed that fear can be conditioned and unconditioned. Behavior assessment, systematic desensitization, token economies, and CBT were all adapted from behaviorism. Behavior therapy has been sharply criticized by civil rights advocates, who point out that prisoners and mental patients have sometimes been subjected to behavior modification programs against their will. However, behavior therapy is growing rapidly in popularity and has produced useful treatments for a variety of human illnesses and problems. That said, typically behavior modification is used as a portion of a treatment profile and does not occur in a vacuum.

Systems

According to systems theory, each individual is in a series of systems, such as families, communities, and nations. Understanding how these systems work for specific illnesses and specific people can provide new ways to more effectively treat them. **General Systems Theory** explains the complex interactions of all types of systems, including living systems, family systems, community systems, and even solar systems.

Postmodern Approaches

There are two main postmodern approaches that influence counseling: narrative therapy and solution-focused brief therapy. In **narrative therapy**, the counselor helps the client to deconstruct problem-saturated stories and construct new narratives that are more adaptive and positive. The underlying premises are that realities are socially constructed; they are constituted through language; and they are organized and maintained through narrative, or the stories that we tell ourselves. Therapists can look for thin and thick stories, and for exceptions to these stories as well. They also need to be respectful, curious, and ask questions about what they are hearing.

In **solution-focused brief therapy (SFBT)**, the main focus is moving quickly to solve a client's problem. This school of thought rejected the disease model of mental illness that was prominent at the time and believed that clients could work quickly to reach their goals. It is a pragmatic, optimistic, and future-oriented type of treatment, and tries to quickly find exceptions to client problems. In fact, this type of therapy is often completed in under six sessions.

The six stages of SFBT are as follows:
- **Stage 0:** Pre-Session Change
- **Stage 1:** Forming a Collaborative Relationship
- **Stage 2:** Describing the Problem
- **Stage 3:** Establishing Preferred Goals
- **Stage 4:** Problem-to-Solution Focus
- **Stage 5:** Reaching Preferred Goals
- **Stage 6:** Ending Therapy

Currently, about 25% of therapists identify themselves as using a purely integrative approach that pulls from several theoretical backgrounds.

SOCIAL AND CULTURAL FOUNDATIONS

As counseling involves working with others, it is important to consider the contributions of culture and other social issues when discussing the field of counseling. In addition, counseling can be seen as a form of social policy—it is, in fact, a way to help others or provide services.

Social policy is defined as the guidelines, principles, legislation, and activities that affect the living conditions conducive to human welfare. All social policies are viewed as plans of action and strategies for providing services. Social policy is problem-oriented—it seeks to improve an existing or anticipated condition. It is also action-oriented—that is, it outlines or describes programs that seek to affect change. It's focused on either individuals or groups, and making social policy involves making choices regarding the extent of changes to be made. The purpose of social policy is to improve the lives of people, and it affects most, if not all, people in society in every aspect of their daily existence. Complete agreement about social needs and the appropriate ways in which our society should meet those needs (and the role of human services workers, like counselors) is unlikely. Due to this, it's important to decide who should receive services and when, and to make these decisions in a culturally sensitive way.

Multicultural Issues

Multicultural issues are directly related to counseling in a multitude of ways. First, clients can come from any of a number of diverse backgrounds, which is important to keep in mind when providing treatment. Second, the experience of living in a multicultural world as a member of a minority group is one reason that an individual could be seeking treatment from a counselor. The effective cross-cultural counselor has knowledge of the group from which the client comes, so as to not jump to conclusions about the client's thoughts or actions.

It's important to mention that counseling approaches themselves could be biased. Many theories were development by white men of European heritage, and their values impacted their theories. Some of these included the important of individualism, the expression of feelings, the idea that you can search within the "self" to find the truth, and the belief that if an individual works hard, that individual will succeed. Additionally, they believed that external factors had little impact on internal psychological states. There is heightened awareness now of taking into account other cultures and becoming more multiculturally sensitive in our theories, and luckily, many of theories can be adapted to address these issues. In addition, don't forget that each individual counselor's biases can interact with existing bias in theories in a multitude of ways.

Research indicates that counseling is not working for many in the United States. Minority clients are frequently misunderstood, are often misdiagnosed, and tend to find therapy less helpful. They are likely to terminate the process more quickly than others. Counselors may not be helpful to clients because they believe in the "melting pot" myth and cannot discuss life in the United States as it is today. Sometimes, they may also have incongruent expectations about counseling, de emphasize the impact of social forces, or unfortunately, hold an ethnocentric worldview. They can also be ignorant of their own racist attitudes and prejudices or of institutional racism in general. Counselors can also misunderstand cultural differences in the expression of symptomatology or misjudge the accuracy of assessment and research procedures.

Using the RESPECTFUL method is a way for counselors to keep factors in mind that they should be aware of when working with a client:

> R– Religious/spiritual identity
>
> E – Economic class background
>
> S – Sexual identity
>
> P – Psychological development
>
> E – Ethnic/racial identity
>
> C – Chronological disposition
>
> T – Trauma and other threats to their personal well-being
>
> F – Family history
>
> U – Unique physical characteristics
>
> L – Language and location of residence

Sensitivity to multicultural issues has led to the creation of new standards for counselors, as they are expected to treat their clients from a variety of backgrounds with respect, and also to understand that struggles with life changes, stress, and work are all affected by the specific culture where they take place. Multicultural counseling even has its own professional association, the **Association for Multicultural Counseling and Development (AMCD)**.

There are new multicultural counseling competencies, put out by the AMCD, stating that counselors should be aware of their own background and resultant biases, that they will seek to learn about the cultures and worldviews of others, and that they will use culturally sensitive counseling methods when working with clients, and these values have also been incorporated into the Ethical Code.

Assessment standards used by counselors have been adjusted to address the fact that not all assessments are unbiased when looking at those from minority backgrounds, and advocacy standards, encouraging counselors to speak out for equal access and rights for diverse groups, have been strengthened. Multiculturalism has been infused into training programs, so students learning about the counseling profession will begin with a more encompassing view before starting to learn specifics of counseling methods and theories.

It's especially important to keep the legal issues and trends in mind when it comes to issues related to multiculturalism, as new legal precedents are set frequently, and social norms, which can affect clients and counselors alike, are constantly in flux. Multicultural counseling can be viewed as the development of counselor competencies to maximize effectiveness in their work with all clients; it is integrated throughout the field at this time.

Discrimination Issues

Next, let's move to a discussion of issues related to discrimination that need to be kept in mind when it comes to human services in general. Currently, over one-third of Americans are racial and ethnic minorities, and that number is only increasing over time. A **minority** is any person or group of people who are being singled out because of their cultural or physical characteristics and are being systematically oppressed by those in positions of power.

Along with this, there are changing religious demographics and changes in gender identity happening at higher rates than seen previously. All of this combined means that individuals in counseling need to have an increased sensitivity to people from different groups. Even the DSM has gotten an update; in the DSM-5, the term "mentally retarded" was replaced with "intellectual disability" in order to be more inclusive.

While this chapter will not get into the specifics of these issues, it is the case that many racial and ethnic minorities have encountered laws restricting their access to work, an education, adequate healthcare, and more throughout American history, and the current environment for these individuals, though it is better in some ways, is by no means free from issues. Values and morals are going to differ from group to group, and it is important for the counselor to find out about their clients' specific backgrounds before making generalizations. It is also the case that for certain groups, mental health issues and other social problems, like alcohol abuse, are happening at higher rates than those seen in the general population.

Counselors can aim to work successfully with clients from varied backgrounds by doing the following:
- Starting with the right attitudes and beliefs, gaining knowledge, and learning new skills as needed
- Encouraging clients to speak in their own language
- Assessing the cultural identity of the client
- Checking the accuracy of the interpretation of the client's nonverbal signals

- Making use of alternate modes of communication
- Assessing the impact of sociopolitical issues on the client
- Encouraging clients to bring in culturally significant and personally relevant items
- Varying the helping environment

Another important factor to keep in mind is religious diversity. Currently, about 92% of Americans polled report that they believe in God but there's a great variety of religions being practiced in the United States. Each of these religions has its own history and culture; there are also individuals who believe in God but who do not take part in organized religion. In fact, counselors should keep in mind the difference between religion and spirituality; religion is more organized, while spirituality can be thought of as mindfulness about the existential qualities of life.

Counselors should also keep issues related to gender in mind. Gender is now being viewed as a spectrum, with individuals deciding where their gender identity falls in the range of options. Diversity of pronouns is becoming more common, as are behaviors that break so-called gender norms, such as clothing choices or career paths. Counselors can provide **gender-aware therapy**, where gender is central to the therapeutic process. This type of treatment views problems within a social context and encourages counselors to actively address gender injustices. It also respects the client's right to choose the gender roles appropriate for themselves. Another option, **feminist therapy**, suggests that women have unique concerns and are often devalued as a function of male-dominated society. With this type of treatment, there's a focus specifically on wellness.

Sexual orientation is another area where counselors may encounter members of a minority group. Previously, the Kinsey studies found much variability in sexuality, something that has been confirmed by more recent research. Even so, many Americans still hold heterosexist attitudes. In the counseling profession, homosexuality has been normalized, and a statement was released in 1998 by the APA against the practice of **conversion therapy**, which attempted to change someone's sexual orientation. Even so, individuals who do not identify as heterosexual will likely have had similar experiences of being treated as an "other" much like other minority groups.

Counselors may also work with other marginalized groups. One example is HIV positive individuals; currently, over one million people in the United States fall into this group. Many of these individuals seek treatment to cope with living with a chronic illness. In addition, counselors may treat the hungry, homeless, and poor, attempting to help those affected with issues related to their mental health and possibly substance abuse problems. It's important to note that some of these groups cross over; for instance, there is a correlation between race and poverty.

Counselors also work with older adults, a group that has become increasingly diverse over time. Research indicates that as the general US population ages, older persons have a high percentage of mental health needs but attend counseling at lower rates than average. This is possibly due to age-related stigma against seeking help, or financial or other access issues. There has, however, been an increase in day-treatment programs and long-term facilities working with the elderly.

Last, it's important to mention that counselors often work with the chronically mentally ill. In the 1950s, the rate of hospitalization for mental illness was much higher than it is currently. Instead, those suffering from a mental illness are more likely to live and receive treatment in the community, particularly after the **Community Mental Health Act** was passed in 1963. There are also new and better drug treatments, and a general push towards de-institutionalization. Even so, about 20–25% of adult Americans are diagnosed with a mental disorder every year.

Related to this are other disabilities. About 19% of all Americans have a disability. Individuals with disabilities are more likely to be discriminated against, have a lower than average income, or be unemployed altogether. A number of federal laws have had an impact on the ability of individuals with disabilities to receive services and find work, including the **Education for All Handicapped Children Act of 1975 (PL 94-142)**, the **Individuals with Disabilities Education Act (IDEA)**, the **Rehabilitation Act of 1973**, and the **Americans with Disabilities Act of 1992**. Even so, these individuals still face challenges and may seek counseling for support with those conflicts.

Societal Concerns

It is also important to mention social issues that could lead someone to counseling. Individuals can seek treatment to deal with stress, violence, abuse, or substance use issues. While all varieties of counseling can help, for alcohol and substance abuse in particular, there are specialized treatment providers.

Alcohol and substance abuse counselors conduct diagnostic interviews, assessments, and are involved in treatment planning. Treatment settings for this therapy include detoxification centers, residential rehabilitation programs, day treatment programs, therapeutic communities, outpatient counseling programs, and employee assistance programs, along with hospitals. Many states have established credentialing standards needed to become a Certified Addictions Counselor. While each state varies in its standards, most require specialized coursework and documented supervised field experience (an average of 300 clock hours) prior to passing a written exam. This is in recognition of the growing need for support for those suffering with substance use problems.

CAREER DEVELOPMENT

Career development is another area where counselors can work with individuals seeking advice and guidance. Career development is a lifelong process and can involve many life roles. It encompasses the psychological, economic, and social aspects of the person. An **avocation** is an activity pursued by an individual because it gives satisfaction and fulfillment; some career counselors also discuss options in those areas.

The counseling profession started with vocational guidance in the early twentieth century, when **Frank Parson** (sometimes called the founder of vocational guidance) came up with a three-step process to find a vocation. The individual needs to (1) know themselves, (2) know the characteristics of the job, and (3) match that knowledge of the self with a job to find the best fit. Soon after, guidance services were established within the school system.

In the 1950s, there was an explosion of career development theories, including Ann Roe's classification system relying on childhood development and theories by Eli Ginzberg and Donald Super, which were also developmental in nature. The National Defense Education Act also stressed career guidance in schools. In the 1970s, a new, comprehensive model of career guidance became common. These models looked at lifelong patterns of career development and encouraged individuals to make choices that reflected their sense of self. It also examined leisure time and other activities outside of work. It viewed the career process as flexible and changeable. These models expanded through the 1980s and 1990s, and today, most models have been refined for easier use. CACREP includes career counseling as one of its content areas, recognizing its value.

This is also an area where counselors should be aware of ethical and legal guidelines. The **Americans with Disabilities Act** ensures that qualified individuals with disabilities cannot be discriminated against in job application procedures, hiring, firing, advancement, compensation, fringe benefits, job training, along with other terms, conditions, and privileges. The **Carl Perkins Act** focuses on the academic achievement of career and technical education students. The **Rehabilitation Act of 1973** also prohibits discrimination against individuals with disabilities but only in federal agencies; the act predated the Americans with Disabilities Act.

Theories and Decision-Making Models

There are a few theories specifically related to career development. The first, the **trait-and-factor approach**, suggests that individuals have unique traits that can be measured, discussed, and examined. Different occupations necessitate that individuals have certain traits, and the better the ability of the individual to match his or her traits to occupations, the greater the likelihood the individual will have success and feel satisfied. This type of therapy focuses on the interaction between the client and the therapist, encouraging a dynamic process that includes both affective and cognitive components. It grew out of Parsons' early work on career theory.

Another option, Ann Roe's **psychodynamic theory**, views career choices as based on the type of parenting received (protective, demanding, rejecting, neglecting, causal, or loving). Essentially, it suggests that the type of parenting affects an individual's orientation toward the working world. While this theory is not widely used today, it is important because it focuses on the impact of early childhood.

A third option, the **Holland Codes**, developed by John Holland, encompasses six personality and work types: Realistic, Investigative, Artistic, Social, Enterprising, and Conventional. Holland states that most people fall under one category. Determining which type a person is key to finding a job that requires and also nurtures the key trait. In doing so, the individual can find a fulfilling career that satisfies his or her needs.

In Super's **lifespan approach**, career development is an ongoing and orderly process. People's abilities, traits, and self-concepts differ, and occupations tend to be specific for certain kinds of qualities. In this approach, self-concept is a function and result of career development. The change in occupational levels is thought to be influenced by many factors, and career development is assisted by helping individuals to understand and develop their abilities and interests. By understanding development, counselors can pick interventions that assist individuals in their career development process.

In the **social cognitive career theory (SCCT)**, the idea is that there is a dynamic interplay between environment and beliefs, where the choices people make are based on personal beliefs on what they can do. This is related to their family experiences, social influences, abilities, aptitudes, interests, and personality. People are affected by objective factors, like economic issues, education, and discrimination but also by perceived emotional factors—in other words, how these objective factors are experienced.

A postmodern approach is **constructivist career counseling**, which relates to how people make meaning out of the world of work. The counselor tries to understand the client's narrative, or life story, and asks questions to help the client deconstruct the dominant narratives. Sometimes, counselors help clients understand how some narratives are a function of language and influences from the larger societal and cultural system.

Many counselors today try to integrate the various models to provide the best treatment option. Additionally, they take a multicultural focus, and use the **Multicultural Career Counseling & Development Competencies**, developed by the National Career Development Association (NDCA) in 2009, to ensure that they are following the rules for best practice in this area. Many use a **relational constructionist approach**, which assumes that change does not simply reside "within' the person, but rather is a function of interactions with people, including the counselor. It also assumes that individuals can see how biases and discrimination have affected them. This approach encourages the counselor to be a good listener of their clients' stories and to be an advocate for oppressed groups.

In terms of professional associations, both the NCDA and the National Employment Counseling Association (NECA) focus on career development. There are also a few publications that center on these issues, including the *Career Development Quarterly* and the *Journal of Employment Counseling*.

There are some ethical issues related to career development. Counselors should use the *Ethical Standards for the Practice of Career Counseling and Consultation* and the NCDA *Competency Guidelines for Career Development* to ensure they are within acceptable boundaries. There are also specific legal issues to consider, including the following:

- **Carl Perkins Act:** Career guidance for individuals with special needs
- **Americans with Disabilities Act (ADA):** Cannot be discriminated against in job application procedures
- **PL94-142 (Education of All Handicapped Children Act):** Requires students in occupational education programs be given vocational assessment
- **Rehabilitation Act of 1973:** Assures access to vocational rehabilitation for adults with severe disabilities
- **School-to-Work Opportunities Act:** Provides incentives to help schools and community colleges integrate academic learning with on-the-job experiences
- **Title VII of Civil Rights Act and Title IX of Education Amendments of 1972:** Prohibit discrimination against women and minorities in employment.

Career Information Resources

There are a few options for computer-assisted career guidance that counselors can use with their clients. There are some comprehensive computer-based programs, like Discover or the **System of Interactive Guidance and Information-Plus (SIGI-Plus)**. Counselors can do testing on the computer to examine their clients' traits and can even use the internet to find more information. Some options for where to look include **O*NET** or the **Occupational Outlook Handbook**.

HUMAN GROWTH AND DEVELOPMENT

Counseling has had a focus in development for a long time, though the "true" era of developmental counseling started in the 1980s. Starting in 1981, CACREP made development a part of the core curriculum. Developmental models challenge counselors to look at clients from a wellness perspective and to consider what's appropriate and expected depending on the client's stage in life.

Development itself refers to the idea of change over time. It is continual throughout the lifespan, from conception to death, and is generally orderly and sequential. Even though development does mean change, in general, who a person is as a core individual remains the same over time. Development can be painful while it produces growth, which is why many individuals and families seek counseling for developmental issues. In terms of counseling, the development perspective is preventive, optimistic, and wellness oriented.

For counselors, applying knowledge of development can assist clients in making smooth transitions. It can also help clients see how they view the world and understand what motivates them to move forward, while allowing counselors to view expected but difficult transitions as typical rather than symptoms of underlying pathology.

Before comparing the commonly discussed developmental models, it's important to note that there is likely a bias in developmental models. Most have been developed by white males, and most of the research confirming them was also based on white males, at least until the late 1990s. These models may look different if factors like gender, ethnicity, socioeconomic status, or culture had been taken into account during their creation.

Child and Adolescent Development

We will begin our discussion by focusing on development in childhood. Children develop at fairly typical rates, which allows the counselor to know when development is occurring in an atypical way and can lead to a prompt referral if needed. Even so, that development takes place as a child's genetics interact with their environment. Adolescence is the time when teenagers compare themselves to each other as they develop their identity. How individuals identify with his or her cultural or ethnic group can also be explained as a developmental process and is something that counselors should keep in mind.

One influential psychologist, **Jean Piaget**, focused on children's cognitive growth. He believed that children are always trying to learn about the world through experiments and by thinking about what they explore and see. However, he said that children do not think and reason like adults do. His theory of cognitive development holds that cognitive abilities develop through specific stages; as an individual progresses to each new stage, how that person thinks and process things around them shifts along with them.

Piaget said that children develop models known as **schemas** to help them understand the world. These schemas help children categorize information and then later interpret it. Eventually, as new information is processed, the existing schemas must change. There are two methods of change. The first is via **assimilation** where children take in new information that they find is similar to what they already know, so they fold it into an existing schema. The second is via **accommodation**, where a schema is altered when enough new information is learned that a change is needed.

Piaget's four stages of cognitive development are as follows:

1. **Sensorimotor:** Ages 0–2
2. **Preoperational:** Ages 2–6
3. **Concrete operations:** Ages 7–11
4. **Formal operational:** Ages 12 and up

The **sensorimotor** stage lasts from birth to about 2 years old. During this stage, children learn about the world through their senses and motor behavior. Between 5 and 8 months old, the child develops **object permanence**, which is the understanding that even if something is out of sight, it still exists.

In the **preoperational stage**, which ranges 2 to 7 years old, children use symbols to represent words, images, and ideas—they engage in pretend play and language starts to develop. Children in this stage struggle with **conservation**, which is the idea that even if you change the appearance of something, it is still equal in size as long as nothing has been removed or added. In essence, children this age do not understand that a tall, skinny glass of juice and a short, fat glass of juice could have the same amount of juice. During this stage, we also expect children to display **egocentrism**, which means that the child is not able to take the perspective of others.

Piaget's third stage is the **concrete operational stage**, which happens from about 7 to 11 years old. In this stage, children can think logically about real (concrete) events; they are very into right and wrong and can tell you all about the world as it actually is. They do not, however, have the ability to use abstract thought.

The fourth and last stage in Piaget's theory is the **formal operational stage**, which is from about age 12 to adulthood. Adolescents in the formal operational stage now have the ability to deal with abstract ideas and hypothetical situations.

Another way of looking at development is seeing how it develops from a moral perspective. A major task beginning in childhood and continuing into adolescence is discerning right from wrong. Psychologist Lawrence Kohlberg believed that morality develops in stages, much like Piaget's cognitive stages. To develop this theory, Kohlberg presented moral dilemmas to people of all ages to see how they responded. He then reviewed their responses and placed them in different **stages of moral reasoning**:

- **Pre-conventional morality** (birth to age 9) is where individuals are focused on what is best for them.
- **Conventional morality** (early adolescence) is where individuals make judgments based on traditional rules for what is right and wrong.
- **Post-conventional morality** (once formal operational thought is attained) is where individuals make decisions based on personal feelings about what is right, fair, or just in the world. Kohlberg asserted that only a few fully achieve full post-conventional morality.

Other researchers have created models of moral development separated out by gender based on Kohlberg's work, but his model is still the most commonly referenced in this area.

Another method is the **constructive developmental model**, which stems from subject-object theory. It focuses on how an individual interacts with the environment, and consists of the following stages:

- **Incorporative stage:** all actions are reflexive—no sense of self
- **Impulsive stage:** the individual has limited control over his or her actions
- **Imperial stage:** impulses can be controlled but in a narcissistic way to meet personal needs
- **Interpersonal stage:** the individual becomes embedded in relationships; this is the very beginning of the sense of self and of the "other"
- **Institutional stage:** the individual has a very strong sense of self-authorship and telling his or her own story
- **Interindividual stage:** mutuality; share of "selves," difference is tolerated and understood; a self-reflective stage

Erik Erikson's psychosocial development theory emphasizes the social nature of human development. He built upon Freud's psychosexual theory of development to propose that personality development takes place in life stages; as people make their way through these stages, their response is what mainly affects the sense of self. Erikson believed that psychosocial forces combined with biological and psychological factors contribute to the development of a healthy person.

Erikson believed that humans experience eight stages of development over their lifespan, from birth through late adulthood. At each stage, there is a crisis to overcome, with the ultimate result having a major influence on personality development. Failure to master these tasks leads to an unhealthy sense of self.

Erikson's Stages of Development

Stage	Development	Age	Major Event
Stage 1	Trust vs. Mistrust	Birth–1	Feeding
Stage 2	Autonomy vs. Shame/Doubt	1–3	Toilet training
Stage 3	Initiative vs. Guilt	3–5	Exploration
Stage 4	Industry vs. Inferiority	6–11	Start of schooling
Stage 5	Identity vs. Role Confusion	12–18	Relationships with peers
Stage 6	Intimacy vs. Isolation	19–39	Intimate relationships
Stage 7	Generativity vs. Stagnation	40–65	Work and/or parenthood
Stage 8	Integrity vs. Despair	65–end of life	Reflection on life

It's important to note that adolescence in particular is a series of developmental transitions in several areas, ranging from the biological and psychological aspects of puberty to sexuality, intimacy and commitment. Adolescents begin to plan their futures and think about things like whether they'd like to go to college or work, and what kind of career they'd like to have in the future.

Switching our focus to adulthood, it's important to note that of the major theorists, only Erikson really addressed development past adolescence. Adults typically have issues relating to career and family, along with the slow decline of physical abilities. There are also both physical and psychological issues associated with death and dying.

ASSESSMENT AND APPRAISAL TECHNIQUES

Regardless of the theoretical background, it's likely that as a counselor you will take part in testing and assessment as a part of your career. Testing can be viewed as a subset of assessment, which can include informal assessment, personality testing, ability testing, and clinical interviews.

Testing and Measurement

Administering and interpreting assessment instruments is a large part of a counselor's responsibilities. Counselors may consult with others on their proper use, use the assessment results in program evaluation or research, and read about assessments in professional literature. School counselors are sometimes the only experts on assessments in the school system. Counselors will often use informal assessment instruments that they have developed themselves as well, though those will not be discussed further here. The reason for the usage of assessment instruments is simple: testing is another way to gain information about a client.

Testing has been around since 2200 BCE, when China developed an essay-type test for civil service employees. Possibly the most famous test is the IQ test, developed by **Alfred Binet** for the Ministry of Public Education in France. Testing spread quickly in the early twentieth century, and the use of psychoanalysis led to the development of objective and projective personality tests.

- **Objective tests** are closed-response test formats with a concrete answer, like a typical multiple-choice test.
- **Projective tests** are open ended, like an essay exam. They allow the test taker to provide information freely, with few parameters.

The Industrial Revolution led to the need for vocational assessment, which only continued during World War I and World War II. Advances in statistics after World War II made tests more accurate, and the use of computers in the 1980s and 1990s to administer the tests made them work even better.

As far as scoring, what's important to know is that individual raw test scores don't mean much on their own—individual scores reveal more when compared to those of a peer group. This information provides a better picture of how the individual did in comparison to others taking the test under the same conditions.

Statistics help counselors examine the results of testing. **Descriptive statistics**, sometimes referred to as **measures of central tendency**, provide information about the general sample that counselors are studying. These statistics include the mean (the average of scores), median (the middle value of all scores), and the mode (most common score), along with the standard deviation (how much variability there is in the sample) and the range (the distance between the highest and lowest number).

The **correlation coefficient** is another important statistical measurement. The number in a correlation coefficient indicates the strength of the relationship, ranging from –1 to +1. The closer the number is to 1 (regardless of whether it is negative or positive), the stronger the relationship is. The closer the number is to 0, the weaker the relationship is. If the correlation is **positive**, then as one variable increases, so does the other. If the correlation is **negative**, as one variable increases, the other decreases. The correlation coefficient is represented by the letter r.

Correlational research lets psychologists find the strength and direction of the relationship between two variables. Even if a relationship is found, though, it does not mean that one variable causes the other. It is important to note that *correlation does not imply causation*. It could be that a third variable, often called a **confounding variable**, caused the increase in both variables. One common example is thinking there is a positive correlation between ice cream sales and crime rates if both spike at the same exact time in the summer. But that is not necessarily true—rather, it is likely that the weather is a confounding variable that causes both of these to increase at the same time.

Reliability and validity are two important factors that must be taken into consideration with any type of data collection. **Reliability** refers to the ability to consistently produce a given result. In the context of psychological research, this would mean that any instruments or tools used to collect data do so in consistent, reproducible ways. In other words, reliability means consistency, which is the key to a solid experiment. However, even if you have a reliable form of measure, that does not mean that it is measuring your variable correctly. It could be measuring it wrong and repeating that wrong measurement every time.

There are a few different types of reliability. **Test-retest reliability** examines scores on one administration of a test as compared with scores on another administration of the same test (to the same group of test takers). **Alternate forms reliability** compares two different forms of the same test rather than having people take the test twice. **Split-half reliability** compares the first half of a test to the second half of a test to see if the ideas are consistent. Internal consistency measures whether all of the questions on a given test assess the same thing—in essence, does it stick to one topic, or jump around?

Validity, in contrast, refers to the extent to which a given instrument or tool accurately measures what it's supposed to measure. In other words, validity means truthfulness, which is another vital part of data collection. All valid measures are reliable, but not all reliable measures are valid. It's also important to consider whether a test is practical to use in a particular situation. This can be based on the amount of time that it takes to give a test, the cost, and the specific circumstances of the client in question.

Standardization of a test is also key—the administration, scoring, and analysis of all results must be consistent for every iteration of any given test. Most tests need to be evaluated and re-standardized after a few years to make sure that they are still accurate. Tests, such as an IQ test, can be standardized through **norming**, which involves administering the test to a very large population that can be separated into different group types, such as age groups. When the initial results are received, they can be used as norms, or reference scores, and then placed in use the next time the test is administered to interpret future scores. Norms do not tell what a group *should* know, rather they represent what that group *does* know as a general whole. Norming and standardizing a test ensure that new scores and new iterations of a test are reliable.

Another part of a counselor's job when evaluating clients is writing **assessment reports**. These reports are typically a few pages long and include demographic information, the reason for the referral, family background, and any other relevant legal, medical, or vocational information. They may contain behavioral observations, notes about mental status, and any test results. They typically include a diagnosis, recommendations for treatment or other steps moving forward, and a summary. However, problems with these reports include an overuse of jargon, which makes it hard for others to follow; a focus on the assessment process and a downplay of the individual; or just the opposite, focusing too much on the person and ignoring the assessment and results. In addition, assessment reports occasionally are poorly organized or written, or fail to take a position on a given individual's situation.

It's important to mention that a cultural bias continues to exist in testing itself—in both standardized tests and the more open-ended assessments. Standards and ethical codes have been developed to address this issue, including research on what tests to use and what to do if a test does not predict well for minorities. But cultural bias, whether intentional or unintentional, continues to exist.

There are also ethical guidelines for the use of assessment procedures. It's important to keep confidentiality and a possible invasion of privacy in mind. Additionally, clients need to be competent, or able to understand the assessment and why it is taking place. Technology can also cause problems, particularly in terms of the laws related to online assessment. It's important that tests are selected with thought and that the results are released properly, following all ethical guidelines.

Legal issues are important to consider as well, including providing accommodations when needed for disabilities, the right to vocational assessment, counseling and placement for the disadvantaged (Secured by the Carl Perkins Act), and the need for tests to be not only valid for the job in question but also necessary. Tests also need to measure ability rather than disability. Additionally, the Family Educational Rights and Privacy Act (FERPA) comes into play when testing in an educational environment, as it relates to who is allowed to see student records, including results of testing.

Models of Assessment

There are several different models of assessment, each with benefits and drawbacks. **Ability testing** can come in two forms—achievement testing measures what an individual has *learned*, and aptitude testing measures what an individual is *capable of learning.* Both of these can be measured using surveys, cognitive measures, and neuropsychological testing. Neuropsychological tests typically assess cognitive functioning, so they can be used as a part of ability testing; they are also used to check for possible problems in brain functioning.

Self-report inventories (sometimes referred to as **Likert scales**) are tests that can be used to assess personality via multiple-choice items or numbered scales. For example, an individual will be given a scenario or a statement and then be asked to select answers that range from 1 (strongly disagree) to 5 (strongly agree)

The **Minnesota Multiphasic Personality Inventory (MMPI)** was first published in 1943 (with 504 questions), then updated to the MMPI-2 in 1989 (with 567 questions), then finally revised again more recently in 2008 to the MMPI-2-RF (with 338 questions). Originally developed to help diagnose psychological disorders, the MMPI is now used for occupational screening, and in college, career, and marital counseling.

Projective testing is a method often used to assess unconscious processes. In this assessment, a series of ambiguous images or open-ended words is shown. The person being tested is prompted to respond to the given words, scenario, or image with the response that first comes to mind. Some examples of projective tests are the Rorschach Inkblot Test, the Thematic Apperception Test (TAT), the Contemporized-Themes Concerning Blacks test, the TEMAS (Tell-Me-A-Story), and the Rotter Incomplete Sentence Blank (RISB).

An **informal assessment** includes the counselor's observation of the client, the use of any rating scales or classification systems, and an overall environmental assessment of the client's well-being. In addition, this assessment can include information from records and/or personal documents or contain a performance-based assessment.

Another important tool for a counselor is the **clinical interview**. This begins by setting the tone for the type of information that will be covered during the assessment process and allows the client to become desensitized to sharing personal information in this setting. It allows the counselor to observe the nonverbal cues being given by the client as the client answers the questions and provides an opportunity to learn about any problems firsthand. Interviews give the client and the counselor the chance to see if they can work well together.

Diagnostic and Statistical Manual for Mental Disorders (DSM-5)

The Diagnostic and Statistical Manual of Mental Disorders (DSM) gives clinicians in the Unites States a reference and a tool to help understand how patients deviate from typical behavior. The 5th edition (known as DSM-5) was published in May 2013. Counselors use the DSM-5 to diagnose their patients with any sort of mental illness. It's vital to keep in mind that the DSM-5 is a classification system, rather than a true diagnostic tool. This means that it allows the counselor to meet with a client, learn about the client, and perhaps use an assessment tool to gather information. After that, counselors can take that information and see where the client would fall in terms of a diagnosis. It does not, however, tell the counselor or the client any information about the cause of the symptoms, and it, at best, provides a suggestion for how to treat the client and the symptoms. Mental illness cannot truly be "cured"—but it can be managed.

The use of this classification system comes with its own issues, including misdiagnosis, failing to meet the minimum number of symptoms for a disorder but still suffering from an impaired quality of life, falling into more than one category, or poor validity of the categories themselves.

Research in this area has pointed out these problems over the years, but has not yet found a solution, which is why it is important for counselors to keep this in mind as they refer to the DSM-5 as a professional tool.

SUMMING IT UP

- **"Helping"** in prehistoric and ancient times can be seen as a precursor to the human services work today, and this includes the empirical studies of the Ancient Greeks and Romans, the Christian church's human services of the Middle Ages, and the physical and mental health services of the Renaissance.
- The **Elizabethan Poor Law of 1601** established a system in England that provided care for the poor, while the **humanitarian reform** and the **moral treatment movement** of the 1770s and early 1780s resulted in more professionalized services.
- **Sigmund Freud's theories** concerning human behavior were widely accepted by the 1920s and 1930s.
- **Medication** started to be used to control patient behavior in the early 1950s.
- **Counselors** offer possible alternatives and solutions to specific problems such as alcohol and drug addiction, child abuse, reaching career and academic objectives, and dealing with various marital, family, and spiritual issues.
- Counselors may work with clients in **group therapy, family counseling, or individual counseling settings**.
- The **therapeutic alliance** is the bond between the therapist and client and the means by which the therapist effects beneficial change in the client; it is the most powerful factor in the process of healing through counseling.
- **Counselor characteristics and skills** commonly related to successful treatment and the formation of the therapeutic alliance include empathy, acceptance, genuineness, cultural competence, and the ability to embrace a wellness perspective and find a theory that "fits" their individual personality and style.
- **Ethical and legal issues related to counseling** include the duty to maintain confidentiality yet report suspected abuse of children or the elderly to the proper authorities and keep tabs on one's own mental and physical health and seek treatment as needed.
- **Approaches to counseling** include **psychodynamic** (the idea that humans are often unaware of what underlies their emotions and behavior), **humanistic and experiential** (which deals with the struggles of living and how humans construct meaning in their lives), and **cognitive-behavioral** (which includes classical conditioning, operant conditioning, modeling or social learning theory, and cognitive structures and the elimination of illogical thinking) theories.

- **Cultural and social issues** can have an impact on counseling, so the counselor must take issues related to multiculturalism, discrimination, religion, gender-awareness, and society into account when treating a client.
- **Career development** involves working with clients seeking guidance regarding psychological, economic, and social concerns.
- **Theories related to career development** include the **trait-and-factor approach** (which suggests that individuals have unique traits that can be measured, discussed, and examined), **Ann Roe's psychodynamic theory** (which views career choices as based on the type of parenting received), **Holland's personality theory** (which encompasses five personality and work types), **lifespan approach** (which views career development as an ongoing and orderly process), **social cognitive career theory** (which examines the influence of beliefs and abilities on), and **constructivist career counseling** (which relates to how people make meaning out of the world of work).
- **Developmental models** challenge counselors to look at clients from a wellness perspective and consider what is appropriate and expected during childhood, adolescence, and adulthood.
- Counselors often participate in **testing and assessment**, which are ways to gain information about clients, as long as issues like standardization, norming, reliability, and validity are taken into consideration when designing and selecting tests and interpreting results.
- **Models of assessment** include ability testing, self-report inventories, projective testing, informal assessment, and clinical interview.

Chapter 4

Fundamentals of Counseling Post-Test

POST-TEST ANSWER SHEET

1. Ⓐ Ⓑ Ⓒ Ⓓ	15. Ⓐ Ⓑ Ⓒ Ⓓ	29. Ⓐ Ⓑ Ⓒ Ⓓ
2. Ⓐ Ⓑ Ⓒ Ⓓ	16. Ⓐ Ⓑ Ⓒ Ⓓ	30. Ⓐ Ⓑ Ⓒ Ⓓ
3. Ⓐ Ⓑ Ⓒ Ⓓ	17. Ⓐ Ⓑ Ⓒ Ⓓ	31. Ⓐ Ⓑ Ⓒ Ⓓ
4. Ⓐ Ⓑ Ⓒ Ⓓ	18. Ⓐ Ⓑ Ⓒ Ⓓ	32. Ⓐ Ⓑ Ⓒ Ⓓ
5. Ⓐ Ⓑ Ⓒ Ⓓ	19. Ⓐ Ⓑ Ⓒ Ⓓ	33. Ⓐ Ⓑ Ⓒ Ⓓ
6. Ⓐ Ⓑ Ⓒ Ⓓ	20. Ⓐ Ⓑ Ⓒ Ⓓ	34. Ⓐ Ⓑ Ⓒ Ⓓ
7. Ⓐ Ⓑ Ⓒ Ⓓ	21. Ⓐ Ⓑ Ⓒ Ⓓ	35. Ⓐ Ⓑ Ⓒ Ⓓ
8. Ⓐ Ⓑ Ⓒ Ⓓ	22. Ⓐ Ⓑ Ⓒ Ⓓ	36. Ⓐ Ⓑ Ⓒ Ⓓ
9. Ⓐ Ⓑ Ⓒ Ⓓ	23. Ⓐ Ⓑ Ⓒ Ⓓ	37. Ⓐ Ⓑ Ⓒ Ⓓ
10. Ⓐ Ⓑ Ⓒ Ⓓ	24. Ⓐ Ⓑ Ⓒ Ⓓ	38. Ⓐ Ⓑ Ⓒ Ⓓ
11. Ⓐ Ⓑ Ⓒ Ⓓ	25. Ⓐ Ⓑ Ⓒ Ⓓ	39. Ⓐ Ⓑ Ⓒ Ⓓ
12. Ⓐ Ⓑ Ⓒ Ⓓ	26. Ⓐ Ⓑ Ⓒ Ⓓ	40. Ⓐ Ⓑ Ⓒ Ⓓ
13. Ⓐ Ⓑ Ⓒ Ⓓ	27. Ⓐ Ⓑ Ⓒ Ⓓ	41. Ⓐ Ⓑ Ⓒ Ⓓ
14. Ⓐ Ⓑ Ⓒ Ⓓ	28. Ⓐ Ⓑ Ⓒ Ⓓ	42. Ⓐ Ⓑ Ⓒ Ⓓ

43. Ⓐ Ⓑ Ⓒ Ⓓ   49. Ⓐ Ⓑ Ⓒ Ⓓ   55. Ⓐ Ⓑ Ⓒ Ⓓ

44. Ⓐ Ⓑ Ⓒ Ⓓ   50. Ⓐ Ⓑ Ⓒ Ⓓ   56. Ⓐ Ⓑ Ⓒ Ⓓ

45. Ⓐ Ⓑ Ⓒ Ⓓ   51. Ⓐ Ⓑ Ⓒ Ⓓ   57. Ⓐ Ⓑ Ⓒ Ⓓ

46. Ⓐ Ⓑ Ⓒ Ⓓ   52. Ⓐ Ⓑ Ⓒ Ⓓ   58. Ⓐ Ⓑ Ⓒ Ⓓ

47. Ⓐ Ⓑ Ⓒ Ⓓ   53. Ⓐ Ⓑ Ⓒ Ⓓ   59. Ⓐ Ⓑ Ⓒ Ⓓ

48. Ⓐ Ⓑ Ⓒ Ⓓ   54. Ⓐ Ⓑ Ⓒ Ⓓ   60. Ⓐ Ⓑ Ⓒ Ⓓ

FUNDAMENTALS OF COUNSELING POST-TEST
72 minutes—60 questions

Directions: Carefully read each of the following 60 questions. Choose the best answer to each question and fill in the corresponding circle on the answer sheet. The Answer Key and Explanations can be found following this post-test.

---

1. A(n) _____ is any group of people who are being singled out because of their cultural or physical characteristics and are being systematically oppressed by those in positions of power.

   A. minority
   B. ethnic group
   C. plurality
   D. majority

2. Which of the following typically focuses upon deep-seated, long-term issues; remediation of severe pathology; and personality reconstruction?

   A. Group therapy
   B. Self-help groups
   C. Psychoeducational groups
   D. Task groups

3. What type of reliability examines the relationship between scores on one administration of a test with scores on a second administration of the same test to the same group of people?

   A. Alternate forms
   B. Test-retest
   C. Split-half
   D. Internal consistency

4. The United States continues to be a highly religious country, with _____ of Americans stating they believe in God, and the vast majority identifying as Christian.

   A. 60%
   B. 75%
   C. 80%
   D. 92%

5. When family members are unhappy with one another and then directly or indirectly take out this feeling on a specific family member, that member is said to have been

   A. scapegoated.
   B. attacked.
   C. ignored.
   D. rebuked.

6. Which term was replaced in the DSM-5 with "intellectual disability" in an effort to be more inclusive?

   A. Intellectually challenged
   B. Mentally retarded
   C. Intellectually handicapped
   D. Mentally disabled

7. Therapists who hold _____ have a right to withhold information about their clients.

   A. communication rights
   B. security of records
   C. confidentiality
   D. privileged communication

8. During the 1970s, _____ personality theory of career counseling, which examined the importance of how and individual's personality "fit" into differing work environments, emerged.

   A. Holland's
   B. Jung's
   C. Johnson's
   D. Super's

9. Which federal law ensures parents the right to access their children's educational records, although generally excluding counseling notes?

   A. Freedom of Information Act
   B. Family Education Rights and Privacy Act (FERPA)
   C. Health Insurance Portability and Accountability Act (HIPAA)
   D. *Jaffee v. Redmond*

10. _____ are often necessary after a group terminates, as members may need an opportunity to follow up.

   A. Referrals
   B. Member check-ins
   C. Accountability partners
   D. Homework assignments

11. How we identify with our cultural or ethnic group can be explained as a _____ process.

   A. historical
   B. developmental
   C. societal
   D. familial

12. In more recent years, development has been viewed as a lifelong journey in which there is _____ ; that is, the individual has the ability to stretch and change in many different areas.

   A. flexibility
   B. plasticity
   C. determinism
   D. mobility

13. _____ are the ongoing interactions among group members and between the group members and the leader.

   A. Group dynamics
   B. Group work
   C. Social loafing
   D. Group counseling

14. Effective multicultural counselors feel comfortable asking their clients about the RESPECTFUL aspects of their lives. What does the "C" in the RESPECTFUL acronym stand for?

   A. Culture
   B. Chronological/developmental challenges
   C. Counseling history
   D. Characteristics

15. Freud identified a number of _____ that help people to cope with anxiety.

    A. defense skills

    B. coping mechanisms

    C. coping skills

    D. defense mechanisms

16. Which of the following is one major task of counselors working in the school system?

    A. Providing mental health treatment in the schools

    B. Giving advice on medication for students with learning disabilities

    C. Administering student-run self-help groups

    D. Testing children within the school system

17. Which of the following is NOT one of the six factors related to building an effective working alliance?

    A. Embracing a wellness perspective

    B. Length of experience

    C. The "it" factor

    D. Cultural competence

18. Families often have _____ and idiosyncratic rules, which can be overt or covert, and are partially responsible for determining the nature of the couple or family.

    A. rigid

    B. universal

    C. illogical

    D. hierarchical

19. Roughly what percentage of adult Americans are diagnosed with a mental disorder every year?

    A. 10%

    B. 25%

    C. 33%

    D. 40%

20. Measures of _____ show how much scores deviate in a distribution.

    A. validity
    B. central tendency
    C. reliability
    D. correlation

21. Which of the following is NOT one of the most prominent conceptual orientations of counseling and associated theories?

    A. Psychodynamic
    B. Cognitive-behavioral
    C. Pre-conceptual
    D. Existential-humanistic

22. Which of the following do psychodynamic theories consider to be important in understanding a person's functioning?

    A. The stories that we tell ourselves about the world
    B. Interactions between systems
    C. Observable behavior
    D. Childhood experiences

23. A(n) _____ is a chosen activity pursued by an individual because it gives that person satisfaction and fulfills an important aspect of his or her life.

    A. career
    B. job
    C. avocation
    D. identity

24. The rise of _____ family therapy took place during the post-modern movement.

    A. narrative
    B. brief
    C. sequential
    D. cognitive

25. Which of the following describes how well a test measures what it is supposed to measure?

    A. Reliability
    B. Cross-cultural fairness
    C. Validity
    D. Practicality

26. Existential-humanistic approaches embrace a phenomenological perspective that stresses which of the following options?

    A. The influence of parenting practices on behavior
    B. The counselor's distance from the counseling relationship
    C. The counselor's interpretation of the client's reality
    D. The need for awareness

27. Adolescence is the time when teenagers will compare themselves to each other as they develop their

    A. personality.
    B. individuality.
    C. identity.
    D. character.

28. Solution-focused brief therapy (SFBT) is defined by which of the following lists of terms?

    A. Pragmatic, deterministic, future-oriented
    B. Future-oriented, optimistic, deterministic
    C. Pragmatic, future-oriented, optimistic
    D. Optimistic, pragmatic, deterministic

29. Which psychosocial stage of development occurs during middle adulthood?

    A. Intimacy vs. isolation
    B. Ego integrity vs. despair
    C. Generativity vs. stagnation
    D. Industry vs. inferiority

30. _____ is the most rigorous form of credentialing.

    A. Accreditation
    B. Licensure
    C. Certification
    D. Registration

31. Which legal case led to a decision that mandates therapists to make all efforts to prevent danger to another or to self, also known as "duty to warn"?

    A. *Clark v. Arizona*
    B. *Tarasoff v. Regents of University of California*
    C. *Julea Ward v. Board of Regents of Eastern Michigan University*
    D. *Jaffee v. Redmond*

32. During WWI, many of the first tests of _____ were used on a large-scale basis for the first time.

    A. mental status
    B. ability
    C. intelligence
    D. achievement

33. Today about one-fourth of therapists identify themselves as using a purely _____ approach.

    A. existential
    B. integrative
    C. behavioral
    D. cognitive-behavioral

34. Where was vocational guidance first used?

    A. Hospitals
    B. Schools
    C. Prisons
    D. Mental institutions

35. Which section was added to the 2014 update to the ACA Code of Ethics?

    A. Resolving Ethical Issues
    B. Advocacy and Social Justice
    C. Distance Counseling, Technology, and Social Media
    D. Research and Publication

36. According to systems theory, a healthy system has _____ boundaries that allow information to come into the system, be processed, and be incorporated.

A. rigid
B. permanent
C. semipermeable
D. nearly invisible

37. Which of the following individuals had the most prominent impact on our understanding and use of empathy?

A. Freud
B. Skinner
C. Cattel
D. Rogers

38. Which Gestalt therapeutic technique encourages clients to take ownership of their defensive projections?

A. Empty chair technique
B. Free association
C. Use of "I" statements
D. Awareness exercises

39. Cognitive therapy was developed during the 1960s by

A. Aaron Beck.
B. Albert Ellis.
C. Carl Rogers.
D. Fritz Perls.

40. Which of the following is NOT one of the three core conditions that Rogers believed together were sufficient to facilitate change?

A. Genuineness or congruence
B. Conditions of worth
C. Empathic understanding
D. Unconditional positive regard

41. Which groups attempt to increase self-understanding, encourage personal growth, and try to prevent future issues by sharing mental health information and providing education in a group setting?

    A. Counseling groups
    B. Self-help groups
    C. Psychoeducational groups
    D. Task groups

42. Which of the following measure a broad range of behaviors related to brain functioning?

    A. Individual intelligence tests
    B. Multiple aptitude tests
    C. Special aptitude tests
    D. Neuropsychological assessments

43. Whose theory espoused the idea that every child was born with innate and unique capabilities and is inherently moving toward the future, not determined by the past?

    A. Adler
    B. Freud
    C. Rogers
    D. Skinner

44. _____ thought that each individual has a unique psychological type, which includes the characteristics of extraversion and introversion.

    A. Freud
    B. Rogers
    C. Jung
    D. Cattell

45. What type of groups focus on the education, affirmation, and overall enhancement of existing strengths of group members?

    A. Counseling
    B. Psychoeducational
    C. Self-help
    D. Task

46. _____ Systems Theory explains the complex interactions of all types of systems, including living systems, family systems, community systems, and even solar systems.

A. Inclusive
B. General
C. Prevailing
D. Simple

47. Couples and family counselors who endorse a _____ approach focus on how behavioral patterns and personality traits from prior generations that have been passed down within families.

A. strategic
B. systems
C. multigenerational
D. relational

48. The _____ offers clinicians in the United States a mechanism for understanding how some individuals deviate from typical behavior.

A. PDR
B. ICD
C. DSM
D. CDC

49. Which approach grew out of Parsons' early work on career theory?

A. Psychodynamic
B. Trait-and-Factor
C. Personality
D. Cognitive-Behavioral

50. Which type of family therapy has at its core the belief that it is critical to understand the stories that individuals and families tell in order to help deconstruct how they've come to understand their family?

A. Experiential
B. Narrative
C. Constructionist
D. Solution-focused

51. _____ occurs when a child uses his or her existing way of understanding the world to make sense of new knowledge.

   A. Accommodation
   B. Assimilation
   C. Schemata
   D. Adaptation

52. An empathic person is someone who

   A. has experienced the problem of another person.
   B. treats others with respect.
   C. has been certified as being empathic.
   D. can understand the inner world of the client.

53. From the 1940s through the 1950s, focus shifted to an increased emphasis on understanding the dynamics of social and family

   A. cases.
   B. practices.
   C. methods.
   D. systems.

54. Counselors will often use _____ assessment instruments that they have developed themselves.

   A. cognitive
   B. informal
   C. projective
   D. structured

55. Today, most people who are referred to as "counselors" have what kind of degree in their field?

   A. Bachelors
   B. Associates
   C. Masters
   D. Doctorate

56. How do theories best help counselors and therapists?

    A. They provide a framework to understand a client's problems.

    B. They are necessary to become a licensed counselor.

    C. They give the counselor an opportunity to network with others in the same field.

    D. They give the counselor a series of steps they are required to follow.

57. Before the 1900s, what was the purpose of group treatment?

    A. To assist individuals in functional and pragmatic ways

    B. To provide an outlet for emotional problems

    C. To discuss group dynamics

    D. To examine personality issues

58. The effective cross-cultural counselor has _____ the group from which the client comes. This promotes not jumping to conclusions about the client's actions or thoughts.

    A. awareness of

    B. understanding of

    C. knowledge about

    D. membership in

59. _____ therapy understands the world and its issues as a function of a male-dominated society.

    A. Equality

    B. Gender-awareness

    C. Feminist

    D. Social justice

60. In the nineteenth century, which of the following societies had volunteers visit the poor and attempt to alleviate the conditions of poverty, which can be seen as a precursor to later counseling work?

    A. Social organizations

    B. Charity organizations

    C. Welfare organizations

    D. Family organizations

ANSWER KEY AND EXPLANATIONS

1. A	13. A	25. C	37. D	49. B
2. A	14. B	26. D	38. C	50. B
3. B	15. D	27. C	39. A	51. B
4. D	16. D	28. C	40. B	52. D
5. A	17. B	29. C	41. C	53. D
6. B	18. B	30. B	42. D	54. B
7. D	19. B	31. B	43. A	55. C
8. A	20. B	32. D	44. C	56. A
9. B	21. C	33. B	45. C	57. A
10. A	22. D	34. B	46. B	58. C
11. B	23. C	35. C	47. C	59. C
12. B	24. A	36. C	48. C	60. B

1. **The correct answer is A.** A minority is any person or group of people who are being singled out because of their cultural or physical characteristics and are being systematically oppressed by those in positions of power. Choice B is incorrect because not all ethnic groups are singled out or oppressed. Plurality (choice C) is a term associated with politics; it is not related to culture or physical characteristics. Choice D is incorrect because the majority group is rarely singled out or oppressed, as its members are more numerous.

2. **The correct answer is A.** Group therapy typically focuses on long-term issues, the remediation of severe pathology, and personality reconstruction. Self-help groups (choice B) focus on the education, affirmation, and overall enhancement of the existing strengths of group members. Psychoeducational groups (choice B) aim to teach their members about concepts that could assist them in their personal, work, or family life. Task groups (choice D) concentrate on a single task at hand, and often spend the majority of their time dealing with problematic group dynamics within those groups.

3. **The correct answer is B.** Test-retest reliability examines the relationship between scores on one administration of a test with scores on a second administration of the same test to the same group of people. Alternate forms reliability (choice A) compares two different forms of the same test rather than having people take the test twice. Split-half reliability (choice C) compares the first half of a test to the second half of a test to see if the ideas are consistent. Internal consistency (choice D) measures whether all of the questions on a given test assess the same thing.

4. **The correct answer is D.** Currently, about 92% of Americans report that they believe in God, though not all attend religious services regularly, and the vast majority identify as Christian.

5. **The correct answer is A.** When family members are unhappy with each other and either directly or indirectly take it out on a specific family member, that family member has been scapegoated.

6. **The correct answer is B.** In the DSM-5, the term *mentally retarded* was replaced with *intellectual disability* in order to be more inclusive.

7. **The correct answer is D.** Therapists who hold privileged communication have a right to withhold information about their clients, as that information is protected. Choice A is incorrect because all counselors have communication rights with their patients; this is not related to withholding information. Choice B is incorrect because ethically and legally, all therapists should have secure records. Choice C is incorrect because, while confidentiality is important in treatment, it does not always guarantee that the treatment provider has the legal right to withhold information about a client.

8. **The correct answer is A.** During the 1970s, Holland's personality theory of career counseling, which examined the importance of how and individual's personality "fit" into differing work environments, emerged. While Carl Jung did support certain theories of personality and its influence, choice B is incorrect because he did not apply those theories to career development. Choice C is incorrect because Johnson's views focused on the influence of the situation, as she supported the influence of sociology rather than personality. Choice D is incorrect because Super's theory suggests that self-concept changes over time and develops based on career experience, rather than that the issue is one of fit between personality and career.

9. **The correct answer is B.** The federal law that ensures parents the right to access their children's educational records, though counseling notes are generally excluded, is FERPA. The Freedom of Information Act (choice A) is related to what the government is required to make public. HIPAA (choice C) has to do with the confidentiality of medical records. *Jaffee v. Redmond* (choice D) is related to the confidentiality of the client and therapist relationship.

10. **The correct answer is A.** Referrals are often necessary after a treatment group terminates, as members may need an opportunity to follow up. While member check-ins (choice B) may also be a good option, they will not provide the same ability to follow up for any individual treatment needs. An accountability partner (choice C) assists with an individual's ability to form new habits or meet their goals but does not serve as an opportunity to follow up. While homework assignments may work well to reinforce concepts from treatment groups, choice D is incorrect because they do not function as an opportunity to follow up.

11. **The correct answer is B.** How we identify with our cultural or ethnic group can be explained as a developmental process and is something that counselors should keep in mind. Choice A is incorrect, as something that happens within the lifetime of each individual cannot be described as a historical process. Choices C and D are incorrect because identification with your culture or ethnicity is influenced by society and family but is truly an individual process.

12. **The correct answer is B.** In recent years, development has been viewed as a lifelong journey where there is plasticity, or the ability to change. Choice A is incorrect because development is not viewed as a flexible process but rather more as a series of changes over time. Determinism (choice C) is the opposite of plasticity; it suggests that everything that happens is caused by factors outside of the individual. Mobility (choice D) is a skill an individual gains with development but is not part of development itself.

13. **The correct answer is A.** Group dynamics are the ongoing interactions among group members and between group members and their leader. Group work (choice B) typically refers to a project taken on by a group of people, rather than anything related to how the group itself functions. Social loafing (choice C) refers to the idea that individuals working in a group work less hard than they would if they were working on something individually. Group counseling (choice D) references a form of treatment, rather that the relationships that take place within the group itself.

14. **The correct answer is B.** The "C" in the RESPECTFUL acronym stands for chronological or developmental challenges. While culture (choice A), counseling history (choice C), and characteristics (choice D) are important aspects of counseling, they are not part of the acronym.

15. **The correct answer is D.** Freud identified a number of defense mechanisms that he suggested helped people to cope with anxiety. Defense skills (choice A), coping mechanisms (choice B), and coping skills (choice C) are not part of Freud's theories.

16. **The correct answer is D.** One of the major roles of school counselors is to test children within the school system, whether for learning disabilities or aptitude for a specialized program. Choice A is incorrect because most school counselors do not spend a significant amount of time providing mental health treatment. Choice B is incorrect because counselors do not typically address medication; clients need to see a psychiatrist for that. Choice C is incorrect because while testing may occur in some schools, it is not a common role for school counselors.

17. **The correct answer is B.** The length of experience of the counselor is not related to building an effective working alliance.

18. **The correct answer is B.** Families often have universal and idiosyncratic rules that are partially responsible for determining the nature of the couple or family. Choice A is incorrect because while some families do have rigid rules, others are less structured. Choice C is incorrect because most families have rules that make sense to them, even if outside of the family structure, those rules are confusing. Choice D is incorrect because while families themselves are highly hierarchical, their rules are typically not.

19. **The correct answer is B.** Roughly 25% of American adults are diagnosed with a mental disorder every year.

20. **The correct answer is B.** Measures of central tendency show how much scores deviate in a distribution. Measures of validity (choice A) show the accuracy of an assessment and are not related to the deviation of scores. Measures of reliability (choice C) tell how consistent a measure is, not how scores fall in a distribution. Correlation (choice D) shows how two different sets of scores are related, but not how much scores deviate in a distribution.

21. **The correct answer is C.** Pre-conceptual theory is not one of the four most prominent conceptual orientations of counseling and associated theories. Psychodynamic, cognitive-behavioral, and existential-humanistic are three of these theories.

22. **The correct answer is D.** Psychodynamic theories consider childhood experiences to be vital in terms of understanding a person's functioning. Choice A is incorrect because narrative therapy, a post-modern theory, focuses on the stories that we tell ourselves about the world. Choice B is incorrect because systems theory addresses the interaction between systems in the world. Choice C is incorrect because behavioral theories are concerned with observable behavior; psychodynamic theories are much more interested in unconscious influences and drives.

23. **The correct answer is C.** An avocation is a chosen activity pursued by an individual because it gives that person satisfaction and fulfills an important aspect of his or her life. A career (choice A) is an individual's occupational path; it may not give a person satisfaction or fulfill an important aspect. A person's job (choice B) is simply the activities the individual undertakes to make money; it may not be something the individual wants to do. Finally, while identity (choice D) is related to the selection of an avocation, it is not an activity.

24. **The correct answer is A.** Narrative family therapy came about during the post-modern movement. While choices B, C, and D are other types of family therapy, they did not rise to the surface during this time period.

25. **The correct answer is C.** Validity describes how well a test measures what it is supposed to measure. Reliability (choice A) indicates how consistent a test is, but not if it's really doing what it set out to do. While cross-cultural fairness is also important for validity, choice B is incorrect because it is not the metric by which you decide if a test is measuring what it's supposed to measure. Even though practical tests are important, choice D is incorrect because a test does not need to be practical to measure what it's supposed to measure.

26. **The correct answer is D.** Existential-humanistic approaches stress the need for awareness in the client. Choice A is incorrect because existential-humanistic approaches do not focus on the influence of parenting practices; that is important in psychodynamic approaches. Choice B is incorrect because rather than the counselor keeping his or her distance, it is important to use personal characteristics during therapy. Choice C is incorrect because it is not the counselor's interpretation of the world that is important, but the subjective reality of the client.

27. **The correct answer is C.** Adolescence is the time when teenagers compare themselves to each other as they develop their identity. Personality (choice A) develops long before adolescence. Choice B is incorrect because not all teenagers will develop individuality, though all will develop an identity. Character (choice D) is present from birth, and not something focused on specifically during the adolescent years.

28. **The correct answer is C.** SFBT is pragmatic, future-oriented, and optimistic; it is not deterministic.

29. **The correct answer is C.** According to Erikson, generativity versus stagnation is the psychosocial stage of development that occurs during middle adulthood. Intimacy versus isolation (choice A) takes place during the young adult years. Ego integrity versus despair (choice B) happens during the older adult years. Industry versus inferiority (choice D) occurs during middle childhood, around ages 6–12.

30. **The correct answer is B.** Licensure is the most rigorous form of credentialing. While accreditation (choice A) is also vital, it pertains to the counseling program rather than an individual. Certification (choice C) is an optional process for counselors and is a less rigorous process than licensure. Registration (choice D) is the process by which the licensing board keeps track of counselors and allows clients to file a possible complaint; it is not a part of the credentialing process.

31. **The correct answer is B.** *Tarasoff v. Regents of University of California* is the ruling that established duty to warn. *Clark v. Arizona* (choice A) is related to the use of the insanity defense in court proceedings. *Julea Ward v. Board of Regents of Eastern Michigan University* (choice C) is related to ethics in counseling; specifically, to the need to follow the ACA ethical code when providing treatment, regardless of one's personal beliefs. *Jaffee v. Redmond* (choice D) protects a client's right to confidentiality in most situations.

32. **The correct answer is D.** During WWI, the first tests of achievement were used on men entering the war as soldiers to discover where they would be the most useful. Tests for mental status (choice A) are typically used after an injury or as part of a psychological screening, and they are rarely done on large groups. Choice B is incorrect because in this case, the examiners were interested in what the men in question had already accomplished rather than what they were capable of doing. While achievement tests are considered to be intelligence tests by some, choice C is incorrect because most intelligence tests are more accurately labeled as aptitude tests.

33. **The correct answer is B.** Currently, about 25% of therapists identify themselves as using a purely integrative approach that pulls from several theoretical backgrounds. Existential therapy (choice A) has become less popular in the past few decades. Choices C and D are incorrect because while both behavioral and cognitive-behavioral therapy are popular, neither hit the 25% level when therapists are asked about exclusive use.

34. **The correct answer is B.** The counseling profession first provided vocational guidance in the school system, beginning in the early 20th century with Frank Parsons's three-step model to find a career.

35. **The correct answer is C.** Distance Counseling, Technology, and Social Media is the section that was added to the 2014 update of the ACA Code of Ethics. It was the first edition that covers the ethics of using social media with clients.

36. **The correct answer is C.** In systems theory, particularly as related to family therapy, a semipermeable boundary leads to a healthy system. Choices A and B are incorrect because having rigid or permanent boundaries would not allow new information to enter and be incorporated into the system. Choice D is incorrect because having little to no boundaries is also unhealthy; this leads to confusion about roles and structure within a family system.

37. **The correct answer is D.** Carl Rogers is the individual known to have had a great impact on our understanding and use of empathy. Freud (choice A) is known for his emphasis on the influence of childhood experiences. Skinner (choice B) is known for his focus on behavior, specifically on making judgments based only on what can be observed. Cattel (choice C) is known for work in the area of intelligence, not empathy.

38. **The correct answer is C.** The Gestalt therapy technique that encourages clients to take ownership of their defensive projections is the use of "I" statements. The empty chair technique (choice A) is more commonly used in terms of working out conflicts with others. Free association (choice B) is not a Gestalt technique; it is used in psychoanalysis. Awareness exercises (choice D) focus on understanding the self, but not specifically on defensive projections.

39. **The correct answer is A.** Cognitive therapy was developed during the 1960s by Aaron Beck. Albert Ellis (choice B) developed Rational Emotive Behavior Therapy. Carl Rogers (choice C) developed person-centered therapy. Fritz Perls (choice D) is one of the supporters of Gestalt therapy.

40. **The correct answer is B.** Rogers believed that congruence (genuineness), empathy, and unconditional positive regard were vital to facilitate change in a treatment setting. Conditions of worth were not included.

41. **The correct answer is C.** Psychoeducational groups attempt to increase self-understanding, encourage personal growth, and try to prevent future issues by sharing mental health information and providing education in a group setting. Counseling groups (choice A) typically focus on helping group members cope with life stressors, less severe mental health issues, or adjusting to new situations. Self-help groups (choice B) focus on the education, affirmation, and overall enhancement of the existing strengths of group members. Task groups (choice D) concentrate on a single task at hand, and often spend the majority of their time dealing with problematic group dynamics within those groups.

42. **The correct answer is D.** Neuropsychological assessments measure a broad range of behaviors related to brain functioning. Intelligence tests (choice A) measure general cognitive skills, not brain functioning. Multiple aptitude tests (choice B) check for the ability to perform well in several different areas but are not specifically related to brain functioning. Special or specific aptitude tests (choice C) explore an individual's ability to perform well in a focused area but are not related to brain functioning.

43. **The correct answer is A.** Adler believed that every child was born with innate and unique capabilities and is inherently moving toward the future, not determined by the past. Freud (choice B) is known for his emphasis on the influence of childhood experiences. Rogers (choice C) is the individual known to have had a great impact on our understanding and use of empathy. Skinner (choice D) is known for his focus on behavior, specifically on making judgements based only on what can be observed.

44. **The correct answer is C.** Jung believed that each individual has a unique psychological type that includes the characteristics of extraversion and introversion. Choice A is incorrect because in terms of personality, Freud believed that it was determined by childhood experiences and the influence of the unconscious mind. Rogers (choice B) thought that humans become their best possible selves when they are treated with empathy and respect; he was not as concerned with personality development. Cattell (choice D) is more commonly associated with statistics.

45. **The correct answer is C.** Self-help groups focus on the education, affirmation, and overall enhancement of the existing strengths of group members. Counseling groups (choice A) center on helping their members deal with negative issues or stress. Psychoeducational groups (choice B) aim to teach their members about concepts that could assist them in their personal, work, or family life. Task groups (choice D) concentrate on a single task at hand, and often spend the majority of their time dealing with problematic group dynamics within those groups.

46. **The correct answer is B.** General Systems Theory explains the complex interactions of all types of systems, including living systems, family systems, community systems, and even solar systems.

47. **The correct answer is C.** Couples and family counselors who endorse a multigenerational approach focus on how patterns and traits from prior generations are passed down. A strategic approach (choice A) would not relate directly to the interaction between generations within a family. A systems approach (choice B) would address many dynamics within and around the family system, not only those that are passed between generations. While a relational approach (choice D) would address how family members interact, it would not specifically address any multigenerational issues.

48. **The correct answer is C.** The DSM, or Diagnostic and Statistical Manual of Mental Disorders, gave clinicians in the United States a mechanism for understanding how some individuals deviate from typical behavior. PDR (choice A) is the Physician's Desk Reference and is related to physical disorders. The ICD (choice B) is the International Classification of Disorders and is used in Europe. The CDC (choice D) refers to the Centers for Disease Control, a US government agency that works with public health.

49. **The correct answer is B.** The Trait-and-Factor theory grew out of Parsons' early career theory work, suggesting that there should be a match between a career environment and an individual's traits. Psychodynamic theory (choice A) and the cognitive-behavioral approach (choice D) are related to counseling approaches, not career development. Personality theory (choice C) is broad and is related to career development; it also predates Trait-and-Factor theory.

50. **The correct answer is B.** Narrative family therapy focuses on the stories that individuals and their families tell to help them deconstruct how they've come to understand their family. Experiential family therapy (choice A) takes a humanistic view of this area and does not focus on stories. Constructivist family therapy (choice C) focuses on experiences rather than stories. Solution-focused family therapy (choice D) looks to solve problems happening within the family and is less concerned with deconstructing how an individual understands it.

51. **The correct answer is B.** Assimilation occurs when the child uses his or her existing way of understanding the world to make sense out of new knowledge. The opposite of assimilation is accommodation (choice A), which takes place when an individual adjusts their understanding of the world based on new information. Schemas (choice C) make up an individual's understanding of the world and are what is used when assimilation takes place. Adaptation (choice D) more accurately references an individual adjusting to new circumstances.

52. **The correct answer is D.** An empathetic person is someone who can understand the inner world of the client. Choice A is incorrect because an individual does not have to have experienced the same problem as another person to be empathetic. While it is important to treat others with respect, choice B is incorrect because respect and empathy are different. Choice C is incorrect because there is no certification for empathy; rather, it is a trait encouraged in many professions, including counseling.

53. **The correct answer is D.** During the 1940s and 1950s, there was an increased emphasis on the understanding between different types of systems and how they interacted, including social and family systems. Choices A, B, and C are incorrect because the dynamics of cases, practices, and methods were of interest before this time.

54. **The correct answer is B.** Counselors will often use informal assessment instruments that they have developed themselves. Although counselors do use cognitive, projective, and structured types of assessments, choices A, C, and D are incorrect because counselors do not create the instruments for these approaches themselves.

55. **The correct answer is C.** Currently, most people who are referred to as counselors have a master's degree in their field, though there are certainly exceptions.

56. **The correct answer is A.** Theories help counselors and therapists by giving them a framework to understand a client's problems. Choice B is incorrect because it is not necessary to focus on a specific theory to become a licensed counselor. Choice C is incorrect because while a counselor could attend a professional meeting for an organization related to a specific theory, that is not their most useful attribute. Choice D is incorrect because while theory can suggest a series of steps that a counselor should follow, they are not required to do so.

57. **The correct answer is A.** Before the 1900s, any group treatment that took place focused on helping individuals in functional and pragmatic ways. Choice B is incorrect because during that time, any treatment dealing with emotional problems happened on an individual basis. Choice C is incorrect because before the 1900s, there was little known about group dynamics, and it is unlikely that treatment would discuss these issues. Choice D is incorrect because, much like choice B, any discussion of personality issues would likely take place in an individual setting.

58. **The correct answer is C.** The effective cross-cultural counselor has knowledge of the group from which the client comes. This background knowledge helps the counselor to not jump to conclusions about the client's actions or thoughts. Choice A is incorrect because simply having an awareness of another group does not give the counselor enough background for objective thinking in this way. Choice B is incorrect because an understanding of another group, while positive, does not tell the counselor whether or not behaviors would fall within cultural norms for that group. Choice D is incorrect because a cross-cultural counselor does not need to be a member of a group to effectively treat its members.

59. **The correct answer is C.** Feminist therapy understands the world and its issues as a function of a male-dominated society. While equality therapy (choice A) might sound like a solid idea, it is not a current treatment option. Though gender-awareness therapy (choice B) stems from feminist therapy, it is focused on issues for all genders, not just those related to male dominance. While social justice (choice D) is a vital issue for counselors, it is not a type of treatment at this time.

60. **The correct answer is B.** In the nineteenth century, charity organization societies used to visit the poor and attempt to help with issues related to food, shelter, access to physical and mental health care, and other stressors.